W9-CYC-234

Other Jossey-Bass Titles on Board Leadership:

The Art of Trusteeship: The Nonprofit Board Member's Guide to Effective Governance, *Candace Widmer, Susan Houchin*

The Board Member's Guide to Fund Raising, *Fisher Howe*

The Board Member's Guide to Strategic Planning, *Fisher Howe*

Welcome to the Board: Your Guide to Effective Participation, *Fisher Howe*

Boards That Make a Difference: A New Design for Leadership in Nonprofit and Public Organizations, Second Edition, *John Carver*

Corporate Boards That Create Value: Governing Performance from the Boardroom, *John Carver with Caroline Oliver*

Creating Caring and Capable Boards, *Katherine Tyler Scott*

The High-Performance Board: Principles of Nonprofit Organization Governance, *Dennis Pointer, James Orlikoff*

John Carver on Board Leadership, *John Carver*

Nonprofit Boards and Leadership, *Miriam M. Wood*

The Policy Governance Fieldbook, *Caroline Oliver*

Reinventing Your Board, *John Carver, Miriam Mayhew Carver*

Transformational Boards: A Practical Guide to Engaging Your Board and Embracing Change, *Byron Tweeten*

The Nonprofit Leadership Team

Fisher Howe

Foreword by William H. Luers

The Nonprofit Leadership Team

Building the
Board–Executive Director
Partnership

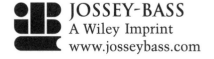

JOSSEY-BASS
A Wiley Imprint
www.josseybass.com

Published by Jossey-Bass
A Wiley Imprint
989 Market Street, San Francisco, CA 94103-1741   www.josseybass.com

Jossey-Bass books and products are available through most bookstores. To contact Jossey-Bass directly call our Customer Care Department within the U.S. at 800-956-7739, outside the U.S. at 317-572-3986, or fax 317-572-4002.

Jossey-Bass also publishes its books in a variety of electronic formats. Some content that appears in print may not be available in electronic books.

Library of Congress Cataloging-in-Publication Data

Howe, Fisher, date.
    The nonprofit leadership team: building the Board–Executive Director partnership / Fisher Howe; foreword by William H. Luers.
        p. cm.
"A Wiley Imprint."
Includes bibliographical references and index.
        ISBN 0-7879-5950-2 (alk. paper)
        1. Nonprofit organizations—Management.   2. Boards of directors.
I. Title.
        HD62.6.H6938   2003
        658.4′22—dc22   2003018766

Printed in the United States of America
FIRST EDITION
HB Printing   10 9 8 7 6 5 4 3 2 1

Contents

Part Three: The Special Challenges of Shared Leadership   101

Resources   161

Foreword

It would be difficult to find a matter more important for nonprofit organizations than the subject of this book. Every public service institution and every nonprofit association needs constantly to grapple with the intertwined problems of governance and management. Museums, hospitals, universities, colleges, and schools, every community service organization and nonprofit association, all face the ever-present demand that they handle constructively the critical but often sensitive relations between volunteer boards and paid executives. Big national institutions and small grassroots organizations, young ones and old, need to find ways for boards and staffs to cooperate, perform assigned responsibilities, and overcome built-in tensions in seeking to fulfill their missions.

For both board members and executives, this book offers three rewards:

- It puts squarely on the table the sensitivity of personal relations between board and executive—the heart of successful partnering—and shows what each expects of the other.

- It reduces the functions of governance and management to the core elements and then points out how board members and executives can share responsibilities and cooperate in partnership to deal most effectively with each function.

- It identifies some special challenges that are most demanding of the partnership—such as the impact of information and communications technologies and new governance and management forms—and sets out in language that all can understand just what board members and executives need to know about them.

In addition, Fisher Howe introduces a novel and helpful feature: in each chapter he provides the "pitfalls" that lurk in practical applications, offering examples of organizations gone astray and the danger signals to watch out for.

In this as in his other books, Fisher Howe does not seek to explore new ground and theoretical concepts but rather to grapple directly and clearly with the practical problems of governance and management. Throughout all nonprofit organizations what do volunteer board members and paid executives face? What do they need to know and how should they address these everyday problems of cooperation?

Fisher has a knack for spotting the key point, synthesizing the essential elements, and then setting it all out in characteristically lucid prose. The book is mercifully short, gets to the point, and speaks clearly.

As he points out, this is probably not a book to be read in one sitting. At first reading, for novices or old hands, it will present an interesting, perhaps surprising, perspective, and then it can be kept on tap for ready reference when new situations crop up, the unexpected appears, or strains in relationships arise.

Although there are innumerable books that deal with nonprofit governance and management, what has been missing is one that deals directly with the personal equation, the partnership cooperation of volunteer boards and chief executives—the glue that holds the organization together and allows it to fulfill its mission. This book supplies that special element.

I have admired Fisher Howe for over fifty years as I have followed his work in government and in the private and not-for-profit sectors. His continuing pursuit of excellence in governance is the mark of this remarkable public servant.

August 2003   William H. Luers
                            president, United Nations Association
                            of the United States of America
                            former president, Metropolitan Museum of Art
                            former American ambassador to Venezuela
                            and to Czechoslovakia

Preface

The leadership of a nonprofit organization is fundamental to the success of the organization in fulfilling its mission. The purpose of this book is to explore the nature of leadership in such organizations and to suggest how leadership can best serve an organization.

Leadership is an elusive term, variously defined, but there is no reason to get hung up on semantics. For purposes of this book, the following is offered as a reasonable definition: *Leadership is having a vision for the organization and the ability to attract, motivate, and guide followers to achieve that vision.*

For leadership in a nonprofit organization, we begin with three underlying propositions. First, the board "owns" the organization: the trustees, directors, or regents stand accountable for all that the organization does. That is their governance and fiduciary role. The board leads.

Second, because the chair is the captain of the board, the strength of the board—and therefore the strength of the organization as a whole—hinges significantly on the effectiveness of the chair as a leader.

Third, the board, for all practical purposes, is helpless without the executive. The executive is the manager in charge of the staff and responsible for carrying out the programs for which the organization exists. The executive also, and indisputably, leads.

Accordingly, the leadership of a nonprofit organization lies with the board, its chair, and the executive. They are the *Leadership Team*.

For purposes of this book, nonprofit organizations are defined as those institutions—other than business and governmental—that are granted tax exemption by law and meet the exemption requirements of the Internal Revenue Code or state statutes. Although Section 501(c) of the Code lists twenty-five different types of such organizations, it is helpful to distinguish only four types:

- Public service organizations—including educational, healthcare, cultural, community service, research, and advocacy organizations—that *exist to provide services to the public*.

- Membership organizations—including labor unions, professional and trade associations, and community service associations—that *exist to serve their members*. Be careful with this category: many organizations that exist for a public service, such as museums and symphonies, have "members" who are loyal supporters; the organization, however, does not exist to serve them.

- Grantmaking organizations—including foundations and United Ways—that *exist to provide charitable funding support to other nonprofit organizations*.

- Religious institutions—which are an altogether distinct category, being in essence membership organizations with an important public service, a spiritual mission.

Nonprofit organizations come in all sizes, shapes, purposes, and stages of maturity; it is illusory to seek a single model of organization or to prescribe one pattern of effective leadership. However, some fundamental principles of leadership are found in all the wide variety. This book seeks simply to identify those principles as they are revealed in three dimensions of leadership: the personal qualities of leadership; the partnership roles of the board, including its chair, and the executive, including the staff, in fulfilling the several functions of management and governance; and the special challenges that face the Leadership Team.

Accordingly, the book's three parts focus on how the leaders of a nonprofit organization function as a team within those three dimensions and their several interacting roles in achieving coherent, effective leadership.

Central to the discussion are three pervasive themes: the critical but often ambiguous distinction between governance—the role of the board—and management—the responsibility of the executive and staff; the often-overlooked but important role of the executive, in addition to managing the organization, in assisting the board and its chair in fulfilling their roles as effective leaders; and the common, perhaps too common, demand for nonprofits to be "more businesslike."

The first of these pervasive themes, the *distinction between governance and management,* is fundamental to the message of this book. Management functions are the responsibility of the executive; governance functions are the responsibility of the board. Drawing the line between the two is often profoundly difficult but is at the heart of the partnership that makes up the Leadership Team.

It should be noted in the functions of management and governance the word "direction" is purposefully omitted for the simple reason that both the board's governance and the executive's management involve direction. Delineating the mixed responsibility for direction is the core element of shared leadership. The board and the executive join in directing the organization.

By the same token, the shared direction of an organization means that the line between the board's governance and the executive's management is by no means always clear. Governance and management are not absolutely defined; they can, and often are, the subject of disagreement, even dispute.

In setting out the elements of shared leadership of an organization, it is imperative first to identify the specific functions of each—the board's and the executive's—and then with each to find the areas of interaction, of mutual dependence. Dealing constructively with the gray areas between the board's governance and the executive's management goes to the heart of what a Leadership Team is all about.

The second theme, the *role of the executive in assisting the board to maintain its own effectiveness*, runs throughout the book.

Regarding the last of the three pervasive themes—being *businesslike*—it is true that in some aspects of nonprofit governance and management, especially financial management and operations centered on earned income, there is much that nonprofit organizations can learn from business. However in many other aspects the differences are major and fundamental. Rather than discuss this theme in each of the elements of governance and management, the book takes it up as one of the special challenges facing the leadership team in Chapter Seventeen, and as an element in accountability in Chapter Eighteen.

Recent years have seen the emergence of a host of academic institutions devoted to education, research, and training in the fields of management and governance of nonprofit organizations, and the inclusion of extensive nonprofit management and governance courses in the traditional schools of business management, public administration, and education. Not surprisingly, with this trend the literature on all aspects of the subject has grown exponentially. Books, periodicals, and conferences now abound on all aspects of nonprofit governance and management and on such subjects as the influence of business forms of governance and management, the impact of the information technologies and communications revolution, and the emergence of innovations in new concepts of governance and management.

This book is not part of this trend in that it does not seek to plow new ground; it is not "on the frontier." Rather it is directed at the practitioner, the everyday board member, the executives and staffs, the volunteers who work in nonprofit fields of every kind. What do they need to know to make their nonprofit organization as effective as possible? What are the challenges they face?

On the other hand, this book may help synthesize the current wisdom on a few central topics for anyone concerned with these matters.

Though leadership takes on no single pattern, the qualities of shared leadership have special importance. Part One looks at such qualities in terms of what the board expects of the executive; what the executive expects of the board and individual board members; and, reciprocally, the personal dynamics among them.

Turning then to the shared responsibilities in a partnership of the board and executive, Part Two identifies six functions of governance and six functions of management. Combining these functions, but taking account of dual responsibilities, the chapters of Part Two explore the partnership roles of board and executive in each of eight shared functions of management and governance: Hiring and Evaluating the Executive (Chapter Five), The Mission, Vision, and Strategic Planning (Chapter Six), Program Direction, Oversight, and Support (Chapter Seven), Financial Management and Governance (Chapter Eight), Marketing, Promotion, and Public Relations (Chapter Nine), Fund Raising (Chapter Ten), Enhancing Board Effectiveness (Chapter Eleven), and Administrative Activities (Chapter Twelve).

Inescapably, a number of challenges confront the Leadership Team—crosscurrents that interact with the elements of governance and management discussed in earlier chapters. But the Leadership Team will also be constantly confronted with extraneous quandaries, such as how to tackle evaluation of organizational performance, how to deal effectively with today's information and communication technologies, the impact of new governance and management forms, or using consultants effectively. These challenges are taken up in Part Three.

Although pitfalls are identified in each chapter, some contra-dictions arise; the more general snares and hazards are highlighted as part of the challenges.

Finally, leadership accountability, a challenge widely misun-derstood, must be shouldered by both board and executive; it is the roundup of the full spectrum of governance and management of the Leadership Team.

This book is replete with quotations. As justification, I can do no better than borrow the words of Roger Soder (2001) in his fine book, *The Language of Leadership,* in which he quotes Montaigne: "I do not speak the minds of others except to speak my own better." And Soder adds, "If it serves our purpose to say it at all, we might as well have it in good form."

———

Everyone I have worked with professionally has helped in compos-ing this book, though they may not know it: board members and executive directors, both colleagues and clients; heads of schools and community leaders; fellow consultants—all have had an impact on my message. If given half a chance, they probably all would want to add to—or change—what is written, but I haven't given them a chance so I can't push on to them any errors of commission or omis-sion. They are mine.

But special gratitude for their help goes out to fellow consultants Peter Szanton, Nancy Axelrod, and Joshua Mintz; to Allison Fine of Innovation Networks; to Jennifer Brown Simon of Venture Phil-anthropy Partners; to Headmaster Jack Creeden of Fountain Valley School; and to my indispensible computer guru, Leslie Power. My warm thanks to editor Dorothy Hearst and her helpful associates at Jossey-Bass. My brother Lawrence Howe has always been there when I needed him-especially for restraint.

Washington, D.C.   Fisher Howe
August 2003

The Author

FISHER HOWE is a consultant for nonprofit organizations with the Washington, D.C., firm of Lavender/Howe and Associates.

A native Chicagoan, Howe received a B.A. (1935) from Harvard University. He started out in business as a traveling salesman for a thread company and then, during World War II, served abroad as a Naval Reserve Officer with the Office of Strategic Services. He has had a full career in the U.S. Foreign Service, with duty in the State Department and overseas in Norway and The Netherlands. Following retirement from the Foreign Service he held positions as assistant dean and executive director of the Johns Hopkins University School of Advanced International Studies, Executive Secretary of the General Advisory Committee of the Energy Research and Development Administration (predecessor of the Department of Energy), and director of institutional relations for Resources for the Future, a Washington, D.C., research organization for energy, natural resources, and the environment.

Howe has been a trustee of several organizations, among them the Pilgrim Society Museum (Plymouth, Mass.), the Fountain Valley School (Colorado Springs), Hospice Care of D.C., the Support Center of Washington, the Metropolitan Washington United Way, and the Washington chapter of the Association of Fundraising Professionals.

His publications include

The Computer and Foreign Affairs (U.S. Department of State, 1966)

"What You Need to Know About Fundraising," *Harvard Business Review* (1986)

The Board Member's Guide to Fund Raising (Jossey-Bass, 1991)

Welcome to the Board: Your Guide to Effective Participation (Jossey-Bass, 1995)

The Board Member's Guide to Strategic Planning (Jossey-Bass, 1997)

The Nonprofit
Leadership Team

Part I

The Qualities of Shared Leadership

Organizations are people. The Leadership Team of an organization is the board, the board chair, and the chief executive. Quite apart from the responsibilities of the board and its members, and of the staff, which are discussed in ensuing chapters, the personal qualities and personal relationships—the ways of doing business—are fundamental to the effective governance and management of the Leadership Team. The compatibility of the chair and chief executive is especially critical to the smooth running of the organization.

Partnerships vary. Unlike the partnerships of equals—in business or law firms—the partnership of a nonprofit board and the executive is one of team players but with different standings in the organization, each with a different role. Consultant Peter Szanton (1999, personal conversation) points out that the partnership of boards and staffs is one of "boundaries and intersections, of borders between governance and management. It is inevitable, even healthy to have some friction and discomfort."

What then are the qualities of leadership to be sought in the participants? The personal relations? They show up in the expectations the board and the executive have in the qualities of each other:

- What a Board Expects of the Executive (Chapter One)

- What an Executive Expects of the Board (Chapter Two)

- What Board Members and the Executive Expect of the Chair (Chapter Three)

- The Importance and Challenges of Personal Relationships (Chapter Four)

1

What a Board Expects of the Executive

What does the board want in the executive, the person to whom it delegates the operation of the organization? Think in terms of the president of a university, the principal of a school, the administrator of a hospital, the director of a museum, the executive director of a community service organization, or the president of a research and advocacy institution. What qualities does the board look for? What character traits? What competencies? And in what order of priority? All are important.

The list can be almost limitless.

Characteristics of an Executive Director

Assume first the executive has a background, a professional competence in the substantive program of the organization. The hospital administrator knows about healthcare. The university president and school principal are educators. And so on. That of course is requisite.

But program aside, what qualities will the board count on in the operating head?

Not in order of importance, though some clearly outweigh others, here is a selected array of qualities, character traits, that the board wants in an executive.

Vision

The executive is a key member of the Leadership Team and as such must have a strategic outlook, must constantly have the long term in sight while making the day-to-day decisions in the management of the organization.

Though the board stands accountable for the mission and future of the organization, it often looks to the executive to stimulate and, with the staff, be fully engaged in strategic planning, to review and determine the mission—the purposes, programs, priorities—and the vision—what the organization wants to be and do in the coming years.

Initiative

Boards don't self-initiate. Board members will have ideas, concerns, suggestions, and will in their turn be stimulators, but they look to the executive and staff to propose and prepare actions.

Boards expect the executive to be constantly suggesting, proposing actions and steps that need board consideration or approval. Put conversely, an executive who sits back as a follower and awaits the initiative of others is going to fail the organization.

The quality of self-starter is high on the list of desirable qualities.

Proficiency

A board expects the executive to be competent not only in the programmatic mission of the organization but also as a director of human and financial resources, to have managerial skills and ability.

The expert manager must be competent with the numbers. An office succeeds only when its finances are ably handled, financial reports are reliable, budgets are clear, and assets are protected.

People—the staff—are the backbone of all operations. An able manager must know how to work with individuals: to lead, to motivate; in short, to manage.

Proficiency is a quality hard to measure. It is revealed in outcomes that take time to show. Experience is crucial. At best, judgments of proficiency are subjective and highly personal. That is why the hiring process is so dependent on reliable references.

Productivity

Here is another elusive quality: some people "get out the work"—produce—while others, though intelligent, reasonable, and reliable, simply don't produce results in quantity, quality, or timeliness.

You can't teach anyone to be productive: one either has this quality or doesn't. A board needs an executive who is productive.

Communication Skills

The executive as a member of the Leadership Team needs to be able to communicate; that is, to write well and speak well. Because the executive is the one who usually represents the organization in the community, communicating clearly and effectively is highly important. Even internally, the executive must be able to articulate views, in writing and speaking, with the board and with the staff.

Openness

Today much is made of the need for transparency in nonprofit organizations; to be open and forthright in all operations, particularly in finances and fund raising. The board wants to have an executive fully compatible with that posture.

But more directly, in the relationship of the executive to the board, complete candor is critical; a mutual confidence that can only flourish with an avoidance of secrecy, a full exchange of what is on everyone's mind.

Falling within the scope of openness, the board must insist that there be no surprises. If there is bad news, the board needs to know it right away, not be uninformed until some disaster befalls.

Responsiveness

The board has every right to expect an executive not only to follow its declared decisions and policies, but also to be constantly and scrupulously sensitive to management decisions that deserve prior information to, or approval by, the board.

At the same time, the executive is a key player in the effectiveness of the board. Without the help of the executive it is rarely possible for a board to do its job competently. Accordingly, the board looks for an executive who is responsive; that is, someone able and willing to do everything possible to help the board be effective.

Those are formidable expectations; it might be said the board expects the executive to walk on water!

The board can use Exhibit 1.1 as a scorecard to see the executive's personal qualities. Apply a score of one to five for each element, with five being the highest. For example, a score of forty would be perfection; twenty-five and above means the executive's qualities are strong. Below twenty-five, the board may want to schedule some needed consultation or training in low-scoring areas or seek a new executive with the desired qualities.

Exhibit 1.1. What the Board Expects of the Executive.

(Score 1–5)

1. **Professional competence**—knowledgeable about
   substantive program   _____

2. **Vision**—balancing short- and long-term pressure   _____

3. **Initiative**—self-starter; new ideas   _____

4. **Proficiency**—manager of people and money   _____

5. **Productivity**—gets out the work   _____

6. **Communications skills**—articulate in speech and writing   _____

7. **Openness**—forthright in all operations   _____

8. **Responsiveness**—sensitive to board directions and needs   _____

Pitfalls

For each of the desired qualifications in the executive there is an undesirable opposite. The pitfalls to avoid are those that go with taking the qualities for granted, or being too casual in insisting on these qualities in the executive evaluation, or at the outset not digging deep enough in checking references on each of these qualities.

2

What an Executive Expects of the Board

If the board will have high expectations of the executive as part of the Leadership Team, so in return the executive has a right to expect some special qualities and strong involvement of the members of the board.

Characteristics of Board Members

It is, in fact, in the interest of the executive to have a strong board and to look for the following strengths in board members.

Participation

Board members presumably attend all board meetings they possibly can. This is the first responsibility of board membership, not to be taken lightly.

In addition most boards have active committees to focus the board's attention on different aspects of its responsibility: to oversee staff, review reports, and prepare recommendations for board action. Board members should expect to serve on at least one committee, attend its meetings, and participate in its work.

Unfortunately, some people accept trusteeship without planning to attend and participate in meetings or committees. Board members must recognize from the outset that if they choose not to attend meetings, their fitness for membership is brought into question.

Occasionally, but rarely, there are valid exceptions. A prestigious name may burnish the organization's community image. Someone with exceptional financial resources may be sorely needed. A prominent restaurateur may offer his facilities for benefits and conferences. Should these be continued as trustees? Probably, but always as a deliberate exception.

The "name-on-the-letterhead" type of board member who feels no obligation to attend meetings should probably be designated "honorary" or placed on an "advisory committee." Someone once explained the word "emeritus": "e" means "out"; "meritus" means "should be out."

In sum, the executive deserves to have board members who willingly accept that meetings are part of the job and give their whole-hearted participation as part of their responsibility.

Competence

Board members bring experience, though the experience need not necessarily be with nonprofit management or governance. The executive relies on board members having skills in some professional field, perhaps in the substance of the programs the organization provides, or in legal, accounting, or public relations spheres. Particularly valuable to the executive are board members with knowledge and access in the fund raising field on which nonprofits depend so heavily.

Team Player

Board members who contribute the most have an open mind and an orderly approach to decision making. They always act in the interest of the organization, without personal agenda or conflicts of interest.

The saying may go, "Board members are unpaid to ask difficult questions," but from the executive's standpoint, good board members' questioning will be done constructively, not simply to get attention and obstruct.

Support

Executives count on board members to be supportive. Internally, board members carry out their oversight responsibilities without encroachment on management. Externally, they are positive in representing the organization in the community.

Here the executive hopes the board member will, as described in Chapter Seven, walk carefully the fine line between support and oversight, helping and watching over, but not seeking to manage.

Contribution

Every board member presumably will demonstrate commitment to the organization by making an annual personal financial contribution, regardless of participation in other fund-raising efforts or in program activities, and will take part in attracting other donations. The executive is not the one to solicit board members' contributions—leave that to peers—but can expect a personal involvement with the organization's fund raising.

Sense of Humor

Members taking themselves too seriously are not much help to the executive or anyone else.

Enthusiasm

Members who relish involvement with the organization—and show it—are always welcome to the executive.

The board can use Exhibit 2.1 as a scorecard to see themselves with the seven strengths of a board member. Apply a score of one to five for each element, with five being the highest. For example, a score of thirty-five would be perfection; twenty-five and above means your board is strong. Below twenty-five, the board may want to schedule some needed consultation or training in low-scoring areas or seek new board members with the desired qualities.

The amusing maxims in Exhibit 2.2, originally suggested by Karl Mathiasen, carry some underlying truths.

Exhibit 2.1. What the Executive Expects of Board Members.

(Score 1–5)

1. **Participation**—attendance   _____

2. **Competence**—experience, skill   _____

3. **Team player**—an open, orderly mind; no personal
   agenda; no conflict of interest   _____

4. **Support**—oversight without encroachment on
   management, representation in the community   _____

5. **Contribution**—personal annual donation and
   participation in fund raising   _____

6. **Sense of humor**—not taking self too seriously   _____

7. **Enthusiasm**   _____

Exhibit 2.2. Some Maxims About Board Members.

1. **Board members don't read.**
   Don't count on them doing their homework.

2. **Board members have no memory.**
   Don't expect them to remember actions decided at the last meeting.

3. **Board members have limited capacity to deal with quantities of
   information.**
   Feed them sparingly.

4. **Having a budget on the table can cause otherwise large-minded
   board members to become trivial.**
   Be careful with budgets.

5. **Board members have an unholy resistance to change.**
   Approach them one member, one change, at a time.

6. **Board members make decisions *collegially*; they participate
   individually.**
   *If you want to get a job done, go to the members individually, not
   collectively, at a meeting.*

7. **Board members and CEOs have to be diplomats.**
   A good diplomat: you let someone else have your way.

3

What Board Members and the Executive Expect of the Chair

The chair of the board is the captain, the leader of the Leadership Team, a pacesetter among peers, a guide for subordinates, the boss.

Qualities of the Chair

The qualities board members and the staff look for in the chair are few, but every one counts. Failing one, the Leadership Team falls short and the organization suffers.

Generalship

The definition of leadership applies first to the chair: having a vision for the organization and the ability to attract, motivate, and guide followers to achieve that vision. All other qualities flow from that simple quality.

Especially in the board's relationship to the executive, board members look to the chair to be the focal point of direction: to build the support for the executive while maintaining the oversight, to encourage or restrain. The chair conveys the board's day-in and day-out wishes and will to the executive.

Involvement

It seems obvious, but the board and the staff expect the chair to be involved—ever present and participating. Something is missing if the chair is distant, letting things go their own way.

Presiding

Nowhere does the leadership quality of the chair show up more conspicuously than in presiding at board meetings. Board meetings are the focal point of governance; they are where information is exchanged, issues debated, and decisions made. It is the confluence of governance and management.

The chair, along with the executive, will ensure agendas that make meetings interesting. Presiding is an art; a chair needs to be good at it. The effective chair will stimulate and restrain, will get views out on the table, keep the discussion germane, but above all be outcome-driven in achieving resolution. Board members can lose interest rapidly with ill-directed meetings.

Bridge-Building

The captain of the team must keep peace among the troops. Issues arise in the governance and management of nonprofit organizations and feelings can run high. The chair must get people working together.

Most important, if conflict arises between a board member and staff, the chair must be alert in order to mediate, moderate the tensions, and settle the matter. That doesn't mean an automatic support of board members; a board member can overstep the bounds and seek to direct the staff. The chair understands the problem, finds the solution, keeps the peace, and keeps order.

Prestige

Prominence alone will not make for an effective chair, but standing in the community will do no harm and may help the organization immeasurably.

Anticipation

A key mark of a leader is the willingness and determination to ensure an orderly succession. An effective chair will arrange for continuity, finding the person to succeed.

A scorecard of chair effectiveness is set out in Exhibit 3.1. It can help the board assess the effectiveness of its current chair and guide it in the selection of the next to lead. Score the current chair or one being considered on a scale of one to five for each quality, with five the highest. A score of thirty is perfect; twenty-five indicates a strong leader. Less than twenty-five and you may want to consider strengthening the board chair with consultation or seeking a new chair.

Pitfall

A competent executive who had suffered from a micromanaging chair points out that it is just as important for the chair to know what his job is *not* as what it is.

Exhibit 3.1. What Board Members and the Executive Expect of the Chair.

(Score 1–5)	
1. **Generalship**—vision and influence	_____
2. **Involvement**—active participation	_____
3. **Presiding**—run a good meeting	_____
4. **Bridge-building**—pull the team together	_____
5. **Prestige**—prominence in the community	_____
6. **Anticipation**—arrange for succession	_____

4

The Importance and Challenges
of Personal Relationships

Recognize at the outset a fundamental hazard in the personal relationships in nonprofit organizations, succinctly pointed out by Masaoka and Allison (1998): "The board-staff relationship is a paradoxical one. When acting in their governing role, the board must stand above the staff and be the 'boss.' But acting in their supporting role, the board members support and assist staff-led work."

Some underlying principles that count in personal relationships may seem obvious but, surprisingly, are too often dismissed:

1. Partnership starts with trust—mutual, confidant, underlying.

2. Trust is built on respect—again mutual, on the part of all board members and the executive.

3. Trust and respect depend on openness. To work together productively, boards and staffs must interact with candor, avoiding hidden agendas and being sensitive to the needs and interests of others.

4. Boards hate surprises. If trouble is brewing, the executive should inform the chair early, not late, and the board as soon as possible. Good news won't be suppressed; bad news is sometimes hard to face up to.

5. Confidentiality needs to be respected. Some board discussions, especially on staff matters or on board personality problems, are sensitive; confidentiality is important.

6. On the other hand, secrecy among a few—side-talks within the board—can be overdone. Cabals and intrigue are destructive.

7. Partnership problems are solved together; be hesitant in seeking unilateral solutions.

Board-staff relationships will vary considerably with the size and maturity of the organization. Young grassroots organizations will usually have an active board, volunteering in program and management activities. Older, bigger organizations will more clearly separate the roles of board and staff.

Clearly the flow of information between board and the executive and staff is key to the relationship and the lifeblood of the organization; it needs to be open and orderly. Maureen Robinson (1998) adds an important warning: "The one indisputable advantage the chief executive will always have over the board is access to information. Insecure executives misuse this advantage to control and limit the board's engagement in issues. Between sharing too little and sharing too much, the chief executive can leave a board struggling to gain a foothold on a topic or swamped in a sea of facts and figures."

But remember, executives are human; although they command a lot of information, they don't always have it at their fingertips. Boards should be tolerant with the occasional staff response, "I just don't know but I will find out." It is altogether legitimate and necessary for a board to ask for information; be careful, though, that questions don't appear to be the basis of criticism.

The partnership will always be strengthened when the chair and chief executive maintain regular, close contact. Anne Towne, formerly executive director of Hospice Care of D.C. and later of the

Greater Washington Area Chapter of Alzheimer's Association, states categorically (personal correspondence, 2000), "From my experience as an executive, I can say unequivocally the effectiveness and the lifeblood of an executive director is wholly dependent on the chair and the relationship between the chair and the exec."

But don't lose sight of the executive's constant burden: The chair serves a term and then changes; the executive stays on and has to adapt to the special needs and idiosyncrasies of each new chair.

Executives also need to keep in touch with individual board members, not only seeking their help when appropriate but also responding to their individual needs and interests.

Communication channels between board members and the staff other than the chief executive should be encouraged but handled correctly. Board members need to know individual staff members and be familiar with their work and their problems. Staff members gain from knowing the board members' outlook. But there are rules that need to be observed.

The importance of a careful balance in the personal communication between board members and staff is brought out by Lawrence Hecox, an experienced Colorado Springs board member (personal communication, 2000):

There are pitfalls when staff communicate directly with individual board members. If the communication is a result of the board's need for facts, and the communication is between a designated member or committee of the board, the dangers disappear as the process is transparent and authorized. If, on the other hand, a staff person or group communicates on its own volition with a board person or group, the contact is likely to be viewed as lobbying and the board may be split into factions of "insiders" and others not in the loop. The safest and usually the most effective means of translating staff needs to the board, and board policies to the staff, is through the chief executive officer.

The only thing to add to that warning is that it applies equally to conversations between board members and staff initiated by a board member. The proper but not necessarily the exclusive link between board and staff is with and through the chief executive.

Socializing among board members, and board members with the executive and staff, is a key lubricant in board effectiveness. Especially with new members, informal gatherings can cement the bonds in a common purpose.

Mutual assistance is at the core of success in this partnership. While clearly the executive has an enormous part in helping the board and its leaders, so also the chair can help the executive in assisting the board to govern effectively: the executive should be encouraged to simply ask the chair for help.

An organization that functions well will have a board that guides and even directs, but also turns to the executive for advice; it will also have an executive who, reciprocally, is comfortable in asking advice of the board.

Pitfalls

Trust is an elusive quality of interpersonal relations. The executive of a management support organization complained that a succession of chairs did not extend to him the requisite trust for him to do his job, when in fact they erred in trusting too blindly and too long as he ran the organization into the ground by ineffective financial management and nonresponsiveness to board oversight directives.

The lines of communication between board members and staff are important and not always recognized to be sensitive; unless carefully handled, they can cause difficulty. Fundamentally, the executive is the "boss" of the staff and translates to the staff what the board wants done. The executive also is responsible for making sure the board knows the needs of the organization. But clearly board members want to know, communicate with, even be close friends of staff members.

Here is a specific pitfall Taylor, Chait, and Holland (1996) have put their collective finger on: "Close ties between the board and constituents unnerve CEOs who are determined to be the board's sole source of information and fear that direct communication between trustees and stakeholders will weaken time-honored lines of authority."

In general it is well to remember in organizational personal relations that board members and executives are personalities. Disagreements, even controversies, are bound to arise among board members and between the board and the staff; they can even be healthy. The important thing is to deal with disagreements promptly, openly, and constructively, preferably without losing a sense of humor and perspective.

Part II

The Responsibilities
of Shared Leadership

The board of a nonprofit organization is the source of control and authority, with the power to make decisions on all matters relating to the organization. The board stands accountable for the mission, overall policy, operations, and the financial integrity of the institution—literally for all that the organization does and does not do. That is governance.

The first thing a board does in fulfilling its overall responsibility is to hire an executive officer to whom it delegates the running of the organization. The executive directs the programs to fulfill the mission, has charge of and administers the operations of the organization to promote and support the mission, and otherwise implements the board's determinations of how the organization is to be run. That is management.

Leadership, then, is the partnership of the board and the executive jointly fulfilling the responsibilities of governance and management. To see how that partnership can flourish, the precise functions of governance and management must first be identified. That understanding can then lead to a determination of just how the board and executive can cooperate, coordinate, and otherwise share in the direction of the organization as a Leadership Team.

While the several responsibilities of direction fall to both the board and the executive, because the chair leads the board and is the principal link between the board and executive, the chair inescapably holds the preeminent position in the Leadership Team.

Turning first to the role of governance, six fundamental areas of responsibility of the board in its governance can be arbitrarily distinguished:

1. Hiring and evaluating the executive

2. Determining the mission and vision

3. Program oversight and support

4. Financial oversight

5. Fund raising—the board's role

6. Enhancing the board's own effectiveness

For easy reference the six areas are summarized in Exhibit II.1.

The management responsibilities delegated to the executive are also arbitrarily categorized as six in number:

1. Program direction

2. Marketing, promotion, public relations

3. Financial management

4. Fund raising—the staff role

5. Administration—including
   a. Human resources
   b. Office, facilities, procurement
   c. Unrelated business activities

6. Board support

For easy reference, the six responsibilities of the executive are summarized in Exhibit II.2.

Clearly there is overlap in the shared responsibilities. The board's governance and the executive's management share responsibility for

Exhibit II.1. The Governance Responsibilities of the Board.

1. **Executive**—the board selects, compensates, evaluates, and if necessary dismisses the chief executive. With few exceptions, the board delegates to the chief executive all management responsibilities.

2. **Mission**—the board defines the organization's mission—its purposes, programs, and priorities—and sets out the vision—what the organization wants to be and do in the years ahead.

3. **Finances**—the board ensures financial responsibility and accountability of the organization by
   a. approving the budget and overseeing financial reports and controls
   b. contracting for an independent audit
   c. controlling investments of capital assets including endowment funds.

4. **Oversight and support**—the board oversees and evaluates all operations and programs of the organization; the board supports the executive and staff; board members are advocates in the community.

5. **Fund raising**—board members contribute personally and annually and participate in identification, cultivation, and solicitation of prospective supporters.

6. **Board effectiveness**—the board assures itself that it fulfills the foregoing responsibilities by regular self-assessment and that it maintains its own effectiveness by diligent attention to the composition and recruitment of its own membership, attendance and participation, committee structure, freedom from conflict of interest, and so on.

some functions, such as finances and fund raising. Moreover, the executive's program direction and the board's program oversight and support are two sides of the same coin. And as important, the executive plays a major part in the board's effectiveness.

Exhibit II.2. The Management Responsibilities of the Executive.

1. **Program direction**—the executive directs the substantive programs—educational, cultural, healthcare, community service, other—in fulfillment of the organization's mission.

2. **Marketing, promotion, and public relations**—the executive directs programs to sell or otherwise provide the organization's services and products to users, members, or beneficiaries.

3. **Finances**—the executive manages and reports on the day-to-day financial operations—bookkeeping, payroll, income and expenditures, and other financial matters.

4. **Fund raising**—the executive provides the initiative and manages and supports the board in programs to raise contributed funds.

5. **Administration**—the executive manages the human resources (personnel), office space and facilities, and any related or unrelated business activities.

6. **Board support**—the executive assists the board to achieve its full effectiveness.

Accordingly, the following functions of the Leadership Team, combining governance and management, are discussed in this section:

- Hiring and Evaluating the Executive (Chapter Five)

- The Mission, Vision, and Strategic Planning (Chapter Six)

- Program Direction, Oversight, and Support (Chapter Seven)

- Financial Management and Governance (Chapter Eight)

- Marketing, Promotion, and Public Relations (Chapter Nine)

- Fund Raising (Chapter Ten)

- Enhancing Board Effectiveness (Chapter Eleven)

- Administrative Activities (Chapter Twelve)

The purpose of Part Two is to show how the Leadership Team can be most effective in fulfilling each of these key functions.

5

Hiring and Evaluating the Executive

The board selects, compensates, evaluates, and if necessary dismisses the chief executive. With few exceptions, the board delegates to the chief executive all management responsibilities, including the hiring, directing, compensating, evaluating, and dismissals of all staff.

The board's responsibility in this area is clear and cannot be compromised. Indeed, no other responsibility of the board is quite so important to the success of the organization as the employment of the chief executive. And nowhere else is the commanding leadership of the chair brought into play as in the selection and relationship of the board with the executive.

But difficulty lurks. The transition in executive leadership can be a difficult and unsettling time for an organization; so much depends on the position and the person who fills it. Not only is the board faced with a challenge, the staff inescapably will feel the uncertainty that goes with a change that touches their security and well-being.

Michael Allison (2002), in a study from CompassPoint, the San Francisco management support organization, found "three characteristic threats to successful transitions for nonprofit boards: (1) boards underestimate the risks and costs of bad hires; (2) boards are typically unprepared for the task; and (3) boards too often focus on the problems of hiring new CEOs and fail to make full use of the opportunities in CEO transitions."

Transition does offer a special opportunity. A thoughtful, diligent board can take advantage of what may be a chance to rethink its mission, its vision of what it wants the organization to be in the coming year, and therefore what kind of a person it should seek to partner with in fulfilling its aspirations.

Considerations for the Board

For the board, employing the executive involves matters of selection, compensation, delegation, evaluation, and separation. It also involves compatibility.

Selection

At times selecting the executive can be simple and straightforward; the right candidate may be obvious and at hand. Often, however, the selection is a complex procedure involving a search committee and, frequently, an outside search consultant to assist. Sometimes, if an organization is in transition, an interim executive may be the best course.

A resigning or retiring executive may sometimes be able to assist the board in the key action of finding a successor, but the presumption is the board will handle this responsibility on its own.

Nancy Axelrod (2002a), in her book, *Chief Executive Succession Planning*, highlights the opportunities transition presents: "The search for a new chief executive is an extraordinary opportunity for a board to have a lasting impact on the growth and success of the organization it governs. If the process is approached as a journey about possibilities, it can be satisfying and even enjoyable for the participants. It also tends to be a labor-intensive, high-stakes, and stressful institutional passage."

As a first step the board must think out deliberately and reach agreement on the qualities they want a new director to have. Executive needs can change. A school or university may need a head or president with fund-raising rather than academic strengths. A public service organization can choose a candidate thoroughly knowledgeable in its programs or one with exceptional management skills. The important thing is for the board to agree before walking the path—and agreement is not always easy. A strategic planning exercise may be called for. Boards must be especially careful in defining the responsibilities of a search committee and the mandate of any search consultant retained to assist in the search. Trouble is ever present in balancing the needs and demands on the board to make a decision and on the search committee to make a nomination. The committee in doing its job inescapably and understandably closes in on its preferences to a degree that can sorely restrict the board's important responsibility to make the actual selection.

One way around the problem is to charge the search committee to put forward more than one candidate, indicating its preferences if it wishes. Another is to make sure the board is kept closely involved with each step and each person under consideration. The two courses are not mutually exclusive.

Compensation

The board determines the compensation of the executive, with the chair having a key voice. The amount of salary and benefits will depend on an array of factors, including the financial health of the organization, the competitive availability of candidates, the pay scales of comparable officials in similar agencies, the longevity and performance record of an incumbent, and the experience of a new manager.

To avoid misunderstandings on such an important matter, it is recommended the arrangement be put in contract form. Although negotiating compensation has to be handled with some confidentiality, the executive's salary will, by regulation, have to be a public matter in the submission of the organization's IRS Form 990.

Delegation

The matter of delegation of management to the executive goes to the heart of this book. The responsibility for management unquestionably is delegated; the problem lies in determining the lines between governance and management—just what comes under the head of governance, what under management—and therefore what is delegated. That is the central feature of each chapter.

But one thing needs to be clear: the board has only one employee—the chief executive to whom the board delegates authority and responsibility for hiring, directing, evaluating, and when necessary dismissing every member of the staff.

Evaluation

An executive deserves to have a careful annual evaluation. A regular executive evaluation process is healthy for the organization.

The procedures for an effective performance evaluation of the executive are at once important and sensitive. Above all the evaluation should be constructive, not negative and fault-finding. Each element of performance can be seen as a shortcoming to invite blame or as an opportunity for strengthening and improvement. The best performance evaluations are those that help the executive be more effective and thus benefit the organization.

As it is awkward and counterproductive to involve many people in such a personal matter, the board as a whole should not try to conduct an evaluation. Rather, the board can set up, probably through its governance or executive committee and with the full cooperation of the executive, a small, select ad hoc executive evaluation committee of respected board members.

The role of the chair in the executive evaluation process is sensitive. Much of the relationship between the board and the executive depends on the ties between the chair and the executive—their mutual respect, their interaction, their day-to-day dealings with the business of the organization. As that relationship may be a central element to the evaluation, it may be important for the chair not to be a part of the evaluation committee, although fully contributing to its work.

The special evaluation committee works in confidence with the executive and then reports to the board, probably in executive session.

Evaluations usually work best if the executive has drawn up for committee approval a set of personal goals for a coming year—more personal than an organizational business plan—to which the evaluation committee and perhaps the board can agree and against which the performance can be judged at the end of the year.

Opinions differ on whether the performance evaluation should be directly linked with the compensation issue. Some hold the compensation of the executive, as with any employee, should flow directly from performance, and therefore the two cannot be entirely separated. Others believe, because the evaluation is designed principally to help the executive in his or her performance rather than make judgments to govern compensation, that as far as possible the two should be kept apart.

Also, because compensation may relate to such other matters as the financial health of the organization, the pay levels of other members of the staff, and comparability with other organizations in the community, it may be preferred to keep the two separate. You can go either way.

Separation

Separation of the executive by resignation may be a simple action. On the other hand, because the decision to dismiss is such a sensitive matter, usually involving the personal relationships of the executive with different board members, especially the chair, it can be fraught with disagreements and charged with emotions that can cloud judgments.

The most difficult decisions for a board arise when the performance of the executive is marginal—good at some things, poor at others; or fairly good but not fully effective in all respects; or when some of the board favor and some are against dismissal. That puts the board to the test. Under the leadership of the chair, the board must weigh the decision with great care and sensitivity. It cannot duck this difficult challenge to its governance responsibility.

Compatibility

Comfort levels and ultimately effectiveness hinge on personal relationships, principally the relationship between the chair and the executive but also that between the executive and board members. Here the qualities discussed in Part One come into play: what the board and the executive expect of each other.

Board members, chairs, and executives do well not to underestimate the need to work at and achieve a genuine compatibility in the Leadership Team.

Pitfalls

Selection: Three Case Examples

The long-time, distinguished rector of a prominent metropolitan church retired. The vestry, rather than make the effort itself, delegated to a search committee the responsibility not only to seek out a replacement but to lay out the specifications for what the parish wanted in the replacement. The parishioners were left out of the process. The selection went amiss and everyone was unhappy. It took two years for the church to recover from the resulting unhappiness. The board—in this case the vestry—needs to take charge and to be clear about what it is looking for.

A large employment training center ran into trouble when the search committee selected its candidate, informed him, and even arranged for a staff welcoming reception to follow the board meeting that would review and approve the selection. The board had no choice but to accept the recommendation; to have done otherwise would have caused major disturbance. When the board proceeded to approve the selection, two board members promptly resigned, asserting that their and the board's responsibility had been compromised. The mandate to the search committee must not impinge on the board's responsibility for the decision.

At an independent but church-related boarding school the search consultant understood the mandate from the search committee to be to find a church-ordained educator to head the school. When three such candidates were presented, the board seemed to reverse itself, claiming it had wanted to consider "lay" candidates as well as "clerical." Clearly there was a major and altogether unnecessary miscommunication with unfortunate consequences. The process had to be repeated with a new search consultant and with hard feelings all around. The lesson is this: the mandate to the search committee must be crystal clear.

Delegation

Most of the problems concerning delegation of authority and responsibility to the executive arise in relation to oversight, discussed in Chapter Seven.

All too frequently, however, some board members, in organizations large and small, seek to impose their will in the hiring or dismissal of subordinate staff. Executives can experience difficulty maintaining their management prerogatives, especially in confronting a prestigious board member with strong views on a staff personnel matter.

Here is an example: The chair of a distinguished national organization demanded the resignation of the executive vice president. The chief executive, who was the president, stood his ground in retaining his valued head of program operations. The board backed the president. The chair—rightly—resigned.

In a quite different and somewhat ambiguous situation, an executive of a prominent public service organization didn't get along with, and took action to dismiss, the person contracted to manage an annual fund-raising benefit event on which the organization depended for a major part of its contributed funds. Here, because of the contractual relationship, the delegation of responsibility to the executive over staff was by no means clear. Moreover, in a fund-raising matter where the board and staff must work in partnership, the executive clearly was at fault in not coordinating with the appropriate board committee.

Evaluation

Most boards understand the importance and are conscientious about hiring the executive. Boards also recognize the sensitivity of dismissal, aware that it can be divisive and test the mettle of board leadership. Many boards, however, dismiss the need for executive evaluation, or treat it too casually, to the distress of the executive and harm—though difficult to measure—to the organization. Executive evaluation can be especially vital when the performance is under question and dismissal is in the wind. The underlying purpose of evaluations must be recognized: to help the executive be fully effective.

6

The Mission, Vision, and Strategic Planning

The board defines the organization's mission—its purposes, programs, and priorities—and sets out the vision—what the organization wants to be and do in the coming years.

The executive has a major stake and will be deeply involved in the board's determination of the mission and vision because these two statements set out the guiding mandate for the management of the organization.

As considerable misunderstanding and some controversy surround the terms *mission* and *vision*, boards and executives must be clear and agreed on what they mean. To be most useful, the mission will be an unambiguous, comprehensive statement of ends—the organization's purposes—and of the means of achieving the ends—its programs and priorities. As such, the mission is an internal matter by which the board determines what the organization does and does not do.

Some people view the "mission statement" otherwise: as a tidy, carefully crafted paragraph for public use in annual reports and promotional brochures. Organizations do need such public relations statements of what the organization does, but those are quite different from the fundamental determination of the course the organization is going to take to guide it in all its operations.

The vision, on the other hand, sets out what the organization wants to be and do in the coming years. It is therefore not simply a list of program goals to be achieved. Rather, it is a statement of the aspirations for what the organization itself will look like down the road: How will it be different? What changes in the mission will be called for? How will it fit into the world around it?

The question of values, an elusive element, may need to figure in the mission and vision. Values are not *what* an organization does, but rather *why* it does what it does and how it goes about fulfilling its mission and vision. Values are the ethical framework that governs the organization's policies and practices, the principles that inspire and motivate it.

Determining the mission and vision of an organization must be seen by the Leadership Team as truly fundamental, setting the course for all its programs and personnel—what the organization will do and will not do. Management consultant Peter Szanton says, "The most important thing about the mission and vision is that the Leadership Team—board, chair, and executive—is totally persuaded about the organization's place and contribution to the community, and enthusiastic about what is necessary to fulfill that purpose" (personal conversation, 2000).

More often than not boards, assisted by staff, will come to grips with the determination of the mission and vision, or periodically review their validity, through a strategic planning process. The chair, more than anyone else, must always be assured that the board and executive have a clear sense of the mission, are enthusiastic about it, and are ready from time to time to make the effort to review and reaffirm its validity. The chair, too, will be the principal link between board and executive in the complex procedures to achieve successful strategic planning.

Strategic Planning

Strategic planning can be a major challenge to the Leadership Team. It calls for mutual understanding and close cooperation of the board and executive on a process that is not simple and on substantive matters that can be controversial.

Most people agree on the importance of strategic planning as a means of determining the mission, the vision, and other important long-term aspects of the organization's operations and as a useful way of pulling together to a common purpose the various elements of an organization. However, everybody has a different view on how to go about it. Here is a set of six underlying principles for a sound process of strategic planning.

1. Strategic planning is successful only when the board "owns" it, that is, when the board itself is fully committed and involved. Though the executive and staff will be fully involved and may usefully take the initiative, the planning itself must not be a staff-driven exercise.

2. Boards can fulfill their responsibility most effectively when they separate the process from the substance of planning. Accordingly, the first step for a board to take is to create a steering committee that, assisted by the executive, will deal with the process—make the "plans for planning"—not itself engage in the substance of planning. Preparing for planning is sufficiently important, complex, and separable to warrant such a steering committee. It can make recommendations to the board on the following types of process matters:

- When to initiate planning

- Who should participate: the full board or a planning team of a selection of board members with staff, constituents, others

- What constituency views and other information are needed in advance, and how to get them

- When and where to hold the planning sessions

- How best to capture the planning outcome, who should prepare the report

3. Strategic planning sessions are most productive when led by an outside professional facilitator who

- Understands strategic planning procedures fully

- Can be objective and outcome-driven in leading complex and possibly controversial discussions

- Can allow board leaders to participate fully, unencumbered with responsibility for leading discussions

4. Strategic planning sessions are also most productive when

- Carried out in sessions wholly separate from regular board meetings

- Participants are given pertinent information in advance and pressed to absorb it, so that few if any papers are brought to or discussed at the planning session itself

5. An important and difficult planning challenge is to identify the few issues that will make the greatest difference to the organization in the coming years, to put full attention on them, and not to be diverted by trying to tackle every problem. Although a steering committee may suggest the key issues going into the planning session, final selection of the issues can usually only be made in the planning session itself after discussion of the external environment the organization can anticipate and a candid look at the organization's strengths and weaknesses. Strategic planning may not find solutions to all the issues, but it should help point the way to finding solutions, and the identification of the issues is in itself important.

6. A realistic and useful outcome of a planning session can be a short report of perhaps only four or five pages, that does the following:

- Reaffirms or revises the organization's mission—the purposes, programs, priorities

- Declares the underlying values that characterize the way the organization goes about its activities

- Sets out the vision of what the organization wants to be and do in the years ahead

- Addresses the four or five key issues the organization faces strategically in fulfilling the mission and vision

Such a report can go one step further and set out some goals— targets of achievement the board hopes to attain.

With such a report, staff will have a basis on which it can draw up an operational or business plan for implementation of the strategic plan.

Pitfalls

The common trap nonprofit boards fall into in drafting a statement of the mission is to think in terms of how it will look to the public rather than whether it meets the need to define the direction the organization is to take and provides a tool of governance and management.

Each of the principles on strategic planning discussed in this chapter presents its own pitfall; planning sessions can stumble by dismissing any one of them.

In addition, the following hazards are ever present in the process of strategic planning:

- Planning sessions go awry when inadequate arrangements are made for writing the report. The facilitator should probably not write the report, although he or she can be helpful in reviewing or editing a draft. Board members should be involved because the board needs to own the product, but staff assistance should be utilized.

- Strategic planning is wasted when the report is too long, too detailed, or too loaded with extraneous, non-strategic current needs and actions. The most useful reports are brief and summarize the consensus on anticipated environment, mission, vision, key issues, and directions for new actions.

- Semantics can be the nightmare of strategic planning. Watch our for jargon and buzz words that love to get into planning discussions. Be sure what you really mean.

- Fund raising and board development are ever-present problems for nonprofit organizations; don't let them dominate the planning.

- Don't hurry the process. It's not easy; treating it with care and respect pays off.

7

Program Direction,
Oversight, and Support

The mission of a nonprofit organization, determined by the board, spells out the programs the organization will undertake, the services it will provide, and the products it will produce to fulfill the organization's basic purpose. By delegation from the board, the executive manages those programs. The management job is to design, plan, mount, direct, and sustain programs most effectively to fulfill the organization's mission, and to report to the board.

The board, for its part, oversees the management, evaluates the programs and operations, and supports the executive and staff. Board members are also advocates in the community for the organization and its programs.

This chapter discusses these roles of the executive and the board in program direction and oversight. In the shared leadership of program direction and oversight, the chair inescapably plays a central role. This role demands sensitivity to the unclear lines between management direction and governance oversight as well as diligence in seeking clarity and understanding as the board and executive walk the delicate path between them.

Program Direction

To fulfill its mission and its purposes, every nonprofit organization has its own substantive programs—the reason for which it exists—that the executive manages. Educational institutions have their curriculum and their extracurricular, student-oriented activities, and, in higher education, research programs. Museums have their curatorial demands, exhibits, and often research and educational activities. Theaters and concert halls have their performances. Hospitals and healthcare organizations have medical services, patient care, education, and research. Community social service agencies serve their beneficiary constituencies. National and local advocacy organizations work for the benefit of the general public. These are all substantive, mission-fulfilling programs that call for expert direction by the executive.

With nonprofit organizations that exist to provide a public service, boards, having defined the nature of that service, will turn over the direction of the programs to the executive, support the executive and staff in that direction, and, though overseeing the performance, remove themselves from the hands-on direction of programs.

Similarly, professional, trade, and labor associations that exist to serve their members retain executives to manage and direct the programs that provide the services. And foundations, existing to provide financial support to other nonprofit organizations, have executives to direct the programs that extend grant support to worthy institutions.

At first glance, managerial direction of substantive programs would appear to be straightforward, quite comparable to providing business or professional services or manufacturing a product for sale. In fact, however, for two principal reasons, directing nonprofit programs can be quite complicated. Programs directly fulfilling the mission—medical, cultural, educational, community service—are themselves complex. In most cases, these services deal directly with people's needs and wants—their personal care, culture, or education—and demand a high order of professional competence in their direction. Executives are put to the test in giving program direction.

Direction of nonprofit programs is complicated, too, because board members with an oversight role often have a close and vital interest in the programs, and, not unusually, a special competence in the substance of the programs. They want to help. They want to influence. As well as being helpful, they can make the executive's program direction difficult.

The size of an organization as well as its mission will make a difference. In larger organizations, including universities and colleges, museums, and major hospitals, the chief executive's management, while delegating hands-on direction of programs to subordinates, is essentially a matter of guiding and supporting the direction, keeping a sharp eye on performance, and reporting to the board. With local community service organizations, on the other hand, the executive will personally direct the programs.

Both boards and executives, therefore, led by perceptive chairs, must go to great lengths to honor each other's role and seek understanding and accommodation when views differ in the direction of programs.

While directing substantive programs, executives also manage supporting programs: finances and fund raising; marketing, promotion and public relations; and administration—and they also are overseen by boards, sometimes quite closely. What's more, executives also have a responsibility to help the board be effective. These matters are discussed in following chapters.

Oversight, Support, and Advocacy

The board controls and watches over the execution of programs, both substantive and administrative, and at the same time individual board members support the staff in carrying out all functions. The two roles, as noted above, can at times be somewhat in conflict—a dilemma that goes to the heart of the distinction between the board's governance and the executive's management responsibilities.

Oversight

The board looks to its executive to direct the programs and to select and evaluate the performance of all subordinate staff. Therefore, except in most unusual circumstances or when the executive specifically asks for a board member's assistance, board members have no business get-ting involved with the hiring, directing, or dismissal of staff.

But it is not that clear. The concept of board oversight implies a responsibility for the outcomes and thus a level of authority over the activities that produce the outcomes. That authority inescap-ably calls upon the board to examine staff actions, sometimes quite closely, and especially the outcomes of staff actions in running the programs. Thus a sensitive gray area exists where the board can eas-ily and perhaps unthinkingly invade the executive's management in the way the board takes on the routine review of operations.

In the normal course boards establish appropriate committees to keep an eye on specific elements of the organization's mission and operation. It is one thing, however, to establish committees to over-see support functions—finances and fund raising—but quite a dif-ferent matter to watch over substantive programs, such as the actual medical care in a hospital, the curatorial function of a museum, the curriculum in a school or college, the social work of a community service organization. Where in these substantive programs does oversight review end and control or dominance of program begin? The line is fuzzy.

An often-heard cliché is that boards, in fulfilling their oversight role, should have a "watchful eye," not a "meddling hand." But in overseeing programs, when does the watchful eye become meddling? No general, marginal line can be drawn that will work for all orga-nizations or all programs. Boards of young, struggling organizations will handle oversight quite differently from leaders of mature, long-tested institutions. Major institutions, such as universities, hospi-tals, and museums will differ in oversight needs and procedures from, say, smaller community organizations and schools.

Central to all oversight responsibilities is the matter of perfor-mance evaluation. "How we doin'?" How well is the organization fulfilling its mission? How effective is a specific program? Questions of performance evaluation present one of the special challenges of shared leadership discussed in detail in Chapter Thirteen.

In dealing with the oversight function, the important point is for boards to be acutely conscious of the fine line they must tread, and in their "meddling" to avoid usurping the executive's responsibility to manage the programs. Harvard's Richard Chait aptly points out, "When boards micro-manage it is almost always because they have not been given a chance to macro-govern" (statement at NCNB Leadership Conference, 1999).

Openness is the road to resolution. Get out on the table any differences in the matter of encroachment. This is an area for frank discussion and understanding between the board chair and the executive.

Ultimately, it is healthy for both board and executive to recognize one overall guideline: while the distinction between governance and management may be imprecise, in every disagreement as to the board's responsibility and that of the executive, the board, not the executive, makes the decision.

Support

Jan Masaoka (2002) of San Francisco's CompassPoint says it simply: "Most nonprofit executive directors . . . need several kinds of support from their boards: praise, constructive criticism, feedback/observations, backing them up to the staff and the community, encouragement, and leadership."

The board as a whole, and individual board members, are expected to be supportive of the executive and staff where they can. Quite apart from the fund raising, which is a direct board responsibility working with the staff, boards, and particularly individual board members, can give moral backing and often direct assistance in staff activities in a manner that is not strictly related to their governance role. Usually the initiative for such assistance will come from the executive or a staff member, but alert board members will often know when and how to offer help without intruding on the autonomy of management.

Keep things in perspective. Although an inescapable tension lurks between the board's governance and the executive's management roles, that should not compromise the support the board gives to the executive and staff.

The real difficulty arises, as was discussed in connection with the dismissal of an executive in Chapter Five, when the board has to deal with marginal performance; is it up to scratch or is it not. There may come a time when the board has to back off from supporting the executive and staff, bite the bullet, and take strong action.

Advocacy

A major contribution board members make in support of an organization is in representing the organization in the community. Board members are prominent citizens. They get about in the community. They are often known to be associated with an organization; their reputation—for good or not so good—rubs off on the organization. Board members can speak out about their affiliation in official or social gatherings, enhancing the reputation of the organization.

Specific public duties are rarely part of a board member's advocacy role, except that some institutions have a speakers' bureau where board members can be called on to speak to community groups, religious institutions, and associations. Nevertheless, occasions are constantly present when board members can speak out among friends and associates about the organization they care for, expressing knowledge and pride in its contributions. This activity needs to be taken as a serious part of the board member's responsibility; it will be noticed and is helpful to the organization.

Pitfalls

Program Direction

For some organizations, the leadership problem in program direction comes into sharp focus either in the selection of the chief executive officer or in the assignment of responsibilities for management between a chief executive and a chief operating officer.

Take, for example, two of New York's most-prominent cultural organizations, the Metropolitan Opera and the Metropolitan Museum of Art. Over the years both have struggled with the choice of either selecting as the chief executive officer a program professional—trained and expert in music or art, respectively—and assigning "support" management responsibilities—finances, fund raising, and so on—to a chief operating officer, or the other way around, selecting as the chief executive officer an able administrator and assigning program direction to a subordinate artistic director. Each organization, having tried both options, has ended up going a different way: the Opera's CEO is a manager-type, its artistic director a professional; the Museum's CEO is an art professional, its manager is chief operating officer.

Healthcare organizations can have similar problems. Hospitals sometimes put a doctor in the chief executive position, sometimes a trained administrator. Universities often, but not always, select a scholar for president or chief executive, but if this position is filled by an academic, the university board will be sure the chief executive has management and fund raising strength as well. Heads of independent schools are usually drawn from faculty, but managerial talent is certainly looked for.

Oversight

The case of the demise of a worthy management support organization exemplifies not only an executive's failure in management, including financial management, but also a board's falling short in its oversight of that management. The board was aware of the financial difficulties the organization was experiencing but believed it was responsibly monitoring the situation through its finance committee, particularly the finance committee chair. However, the finance chair failed to recognize, or to tell the board if he did know, that the executive was misapplying restricted grant monies to other needs, not reporting major arrears in payments to contractors and vendors, and generally living by unrealistic optimism in achieving revenues and contributions. The board, through the finance chair, also failed to keep in close enough touch with its independent auditors, who might have given the danger signals. Incredibly, the board did not even know the auditor's bill had gone unpaid for more than a year. When the organization could no longer meet the staff payroll, it had to fold the tent.

Nor was the board oversight shortfall limited to the finances; the board should have been alerted by the persistent failure of the executive to respond properly to its oversight directives in handling marketing, fund raising, and even program direction.

In general, however, the situation is usually reversed. Oversight board committees often have difficulty resisting the constant temptation to give direction. It is not surprising: board members have an abiding interest in the substance of programs; they are itching to push staff in one direction or another. A museum board member has strong views on an exhibit. A school board member wants admissions policies to be different. A hospital trustee knows something about meeting overhead demands.

Support

A board member who is not enthusiastic about the organization's mission or programs can harm its image in the community if, even unintentionally, that less-than-positive support becomes evident.

Similarly, board members volunteering to assist in program activities don't always understand they are working for, and under the supervision of, the executive, and are not functioning with the authority of a board member.

8

Financial Management and Governance

Though the ultimate responsibility for the organization's financial integrity is the board's, the executive and staff have everything to do with day-to-day financial operations—accounting (bookkeeping) and budgets; audits; and financial reporting—all in accord with policies and directives of the board. Here indeed is where both governance and management responsibilities are brought into full play, the Leadership Team must work together, and the lines between board and executive responsibilities must be carefully drawn.

Here, too, the leadership position of the board chair is critical. In the organization's handling of financial matters, the chair is in the key position, first of all in the selection and dependence on the board's finance committee and its chair.* They will not only be the principal links on financial matters between the executive and the board, but will also be the ones on whom the board will rely in technical financial decisions.

Jan Masaoka (2000) of CompassPoint Nonprofit Services, the San Francisco management support organization, and editor of *Board Cafe*, a free newsletter for nonprofit boards and executive directors available at www.boardcafe.org, emphasizes that "each organization needs to develop a clear and explicit agreement on

---

*The title of treasurer for the board's principal member looking after financial matters is discussed in terms of a pitfall in Chapter Eleven.

how financial accountability will be ensured." She offers a suggested "contract" that board and staff can make (see Resource A).

On financial as on other matters, both the board and the executive have areas in which they have principal responsibility but where both are deeply involved. The problem then is to sort out the combined responsibilities in the following five arbitrarily delineated financial functions:

- Accounting

- Budgets

- Audits

- Investments

- Financial reports

Accounting

The executive—whether alone or supported by a chief financial officer, business manager, or other staff—will keep the books. Essentially that involves handling and recording all income—accounts receivable, earned revenue, contributed funds (both unrestricted and program-restricted), and investment income—and expenses— accounts payable, payroll (including benefits), program outlays, travel, entertainment, and miscellaneous expenses. The board, principally through a finance committee, will assure itself that prudent accounting policies and internal controls are in place.

Budgets

The budget process has a dual purpose. It is, first, a policy and planning document, an instrument by which the board oversees what the organization will do and how it will do it. Thus, in the normal course, the executive will annually prepare a business plan for board approval. The plan will outline how programs and operations will be managed for the coming year to fulfill the board's directives, usually articulated in its strategic plans. The budget is the financial reflection of the business plan.

Second, the budget is a control document, the mechanism by which the board monitors and ensures that the organization is operating within its means and in conformity with directives. As such it is a tool for setting priorities on what resources will be allocated.

Budgets are prepared by staff under the direction of the executive in advance of the coming fiscal year and go through preliminary, adjusted, and final forms. They are usually reviewed by a board finance or budget committee and presented for approval to the board. Executive and finance officers and board finance committees can be the most helpful when they identify and highlight for the board the essential issues that deserve board consideration. It is not numbers alone that count; the policy implications invariably embedded in the numbers determine the direction the organization's activities will take.

The board's budget role, especially as a control instrument insofar as it is determining what and how programs will be carried out, comes dangerously close to a management responsibility, impinging on the executive's responsibility. As management consultant John Carver (1990) points out, preparation and approval of the budget is at the interface of board governance and staff management. In dealing with the budget, boards must fulfill their control and oversight responsibility but not cross over into management by seeking to direct programs or make administrative decisions through the budget process. It is essential, however, that board members exhibit a healthy degree of skepticism in regard to major variances appearing in budget line items.

Audits

The audit is the board's most powerful instrument for ensuring accuracy and honesty of the organization's financial management.

Financial statements are the responsibility of management. Independent auditors are retained by the organization's board and paid to express an opinion based on a review of those financial statements. An audit includes an examination, on a test basis, of evidence supporting the information in the financial statement. As well as evaluating the overall financial presentation, an audit assesses the accounting principles used and significant estimates made by management. The auditors then assert that, as of a certain date, the financial statements in their opinion present fairly, in all material respects, the financial position of the organization and the changes in net assets and cash flows for the year, in conformity with accounting principles generally accepted in the United States.

The key word is "material"; auditors do not claim to find and report every flaw. Nor does the auditors' mandate require them to volunteer views on, for example, expense accounts, investment income, spending policies, or improprieties that may not have a direct impact on financial accounting—things that don't fall within their "generally accepted accounting principles." However, on request and possibly for a fee, auditors will go beyond the basic review and report on those related matters as well.

It is altogether appropriate, therefore, and highly desirable—some say mandatory—for the board, probably through the finance (or audit) committee, to keep in close, direct touch with the auditor, as much as to ask, "Are there any things you see that, from your experience with other like organizations, you think we should be aware of?"

Indeed, CPAs have the reciprocal responsibility to communicate to an audit committee (or equivalent) on very specific points, including any disagreements with management or difficulties encountered in performing the audit.

Thus it is possible for audits to be immensely helpful to the board. Auditors can respond candidly to requests to identify financial and administrative procedures that need examination or could be improved. But they have to be asked.

The responsibility for contracting for the audit is unequivocally the board's, not to be delegated to the staff. Let there be no doubt that the auditors are the agents of the board and report to it.

Investments

Clearly, the board's most basic responsibility is to preserve institutional resources, including the endowment, in perpetuity.

The capital assets of a nonprofit organization can be of two kinds: fixed assets, including property, plant, and equipment; and financial assets, including donations specifically restricted to endowment by the donors and funds designated by the board for capital investment.

Board responsibility for handling financial assets, including endowments and reserve funds, is one of the few areas where the board has a managerial role. The executive and, if there is one, a chief financial officer can be helpful, will certainly be closely familiar with investment activities, and will handle short-term deposits and investments. But the board is completely in charge of investment policy.

Accordingly, the board takes the following actions:

- Determines what funds are to be handled as capital investments

- Defines the investment portfolio strategies, setting guidelines to balance the goals of growth, income, and risk; and determines the mix of equity, debt, or other instruments

- Selects, where appropriate, one or more independent investment management agencies to provide advice and implement investment decisions; and monitors closely the investment performance

- Recommends to the board the estimates of investment returns that will be available for the operations budget; that is, the spending policy

Because of the importance to the organization of its investment funds—when it has them—boards are well advised to maintain undisputed control over the funds, clearly define their managerial decisions with respect to the funds in written policies and decisions, and ensure total freedom from conflict of interest.

If an organization has substantial funds to invest, it will probably wish to have an investment committee, separate from the finance committee, to which it can delegate considerable responsibility for these managerial duties. Although the investments of course deal with money and its management, the function of investing is a highly specialized financial operation, not at all the same as everyday financial management. An investment committee, separate from the finance or budget committee, can focus the board's attention on and sharpen the recommendations for necessary board decisions on these important but somewhat technical matters.

Organizations with major endowments to invest may periodically retain independent experts to evaluate the performance of its investment managers.

Throughout, the executive's job with respect to investments is secondary. But because executives have an important stake in the successful investment of assets, the income from which will be for management to spend, they will want to watch performance closely and assist the board throughout.

Financial Reports

For the board to be kept fully informed on financial matters, which it must be, it will regularly receive several financial statements in addition to the annual audit and financial planning documents, such as the executive's annual business or operations plan and the annual budget. These include the following periodic reports prepared by staff and carefully, responsibly reviewed by the finance committee:

- Income and expense statement (Statement of Activities), presenting current financial activities

- Balance sheet (Statement of Financial Position), presenting the organization's overall financial condition, assets and liabilities

- Cash flow statement showing liquidity status

All of these financial reports, especially the budget, are built upon underlying assumptions—prevailing or anticipated conditions or policy decisions that will or could directly affect the figures presented. Without fail, these must be explicit and fully understood by the board in its reviews.

The board, or finance committee, should work out for itself what formats for presentation of financial information are most meaningful for it and should insist on seeing the financials laid out in that way, as well as any different way the auditors, government agency, or client requires. The board, for instance, may want to see budgets arrayed in program form in addition to accounting category form.

Board members should also be quite familiar with the IRS Form 990 prepared by the executive and filed annually so the Internal Revenue Service can determine whether the organization continues to fulfill the requirements of its tax-exempt status. In addition to being a statement of the organization's mission and program activities, Form 990 gives financial details, including the names of board members and key staff and their compensation if more than $50,000 per year. Form 990 must be available to the public, although the sources and amounts of contributions do not need to be made public.

In all financial matters, the chair will want to be directly involved with the executive and the finance committee, making doubly sure that reports are submitted regularly and accurately and that they are fully understood and approved by the board.

Pitfalls

Budgets

Boards can err in being so aggressive in focusing on the details as to miss the big picture. It is all too common to have a numbers-obsessed board member force the board into so much financial detail that it falls short on its other responsibilities. A favorite maxim (noted in Exhibit 2.2) goes like this: "Having a budget on the table can cause otherwise large-minded board members to become trivial." Which is to say that budgets can be the path for board members to climb into management.

Audits

Too often boards of nonprofit organizations delegate the audit responsibility to the staff. One has only to look at difficulties that respected national institutions have encountered to see where a sound audit procedure might have prevented trouble.

For example, the unfortunate major difficulties visited upon the national United Way organization a few years ago involving the criminal activity of its chief executive in dealing with the organization's finances almost surely could have been avoided if the board had been more diligent in conducting its financial oversight and particularly in taking full advantage of the audit relationship.

Investments

Inexperienced boards run into trouble treating too lightly the need for a rigorous spending policy and dipping too readily into the principal of designated capital funds to meet operating budget shortfalls.

When large sums are involved, boards must be exacting in the care they take to guard against conflicts of interest and to ensure prudent judgments are made on all questions, using all the professional advice available.

Financial Reports

The most common pitfall in the relationship of board and staff on financial reporting is that financial reports are not clearly presented and for one reason or another are not fully understood by board members. Consultant Nancy Axelrod (2002b), former president of the National Center for Nonprofit Boards (now Board Source), finds one of the lessons nonprofit boards can learn from the Enron scandal: "Enron's implosion may encourage more individual trustees to ask themselves: 'Do I understand the true financial picture of this institution I govern? And if not, is it because our financial statements are obscure? Or is it because I've never mastered that mysterious language called fund accounting? Or is it because I choose to completely delegate financial oversight to the finance committee, or the executive committee, or the chief financial officer?'"

Boards must be watchful. Harvard Fellow William P. Ryan (2001) sums it up well: "Most nonprofit financial scandals and catastrophes take place in organizations that have plenty of systems, but not enough vigilant, tough board members willing to raise questions."

As a case in point, the *Chronicle of Philanthropy* reported (Fix, 2001) that Children's Express, a charity that trains children as journalists, found itself with a $2.4 million debt and abruptly ended its operations, closing its offices in New York, Washington, Marquette (Mich.), and Tokyo, laying off all but two people and thwarting the journalistic aspirations of children on two continents. The cause is this: failure by the board to pay attention to fundamentals—ensuring that enough money came in to cover expenses, avoiding overreliance on a sole source of income, and making sure the charity stayed on course after the death of the founder.

Mismanagement

Financial pitfalls of any kind can be calamitous. Mismanagement can take place in any of the financial or other administrative functions. Irresponsibility, malfeasance, fraud can be—usually are—fatal to an organization. That is why the executive in managing and the board in its governance oversight must be relentlessly diligent and open.

It is in the interest of the executive as well as the board to have a strong chair of the finance committee and have the full board contract for and pay close attention to an independent auditor.

One pitfall that is less than fatal but clearly a breach of correct management and probably unethical, is, as noted in Chapter Ten, for a manager to allocate, even temporarily, funds contributed for a specific program or project to expenditures other than that designated by the donor.

9

Marketing, Promotion, and Public Relations

It would be difficult to find a more direct and appropriate approach to the subject of marketing and nonprofit organizations than that offered by University of Pittsburgh's Siri N. Espy (1993):

> Today's nonprofit organizations face a number of challenges and in some cases are turning to business and industry to learn new solutions. Marketing is one concept that nonprofits borrowed from their for-profit counterparts. Many nonprofit organizations, however, are working with an incomplete understanding of the spirit of marketing and struggling with the issue of whether and how to integrate marketing concepts. . . .
>
> Most of us tend to see marketing as a means of selling or promoting what we have to offer, often to an unwilling audience. However, if done effectively, marketing is much more than that. . . . Marketing is:
>
> • A means of identifying what is wanted and needed
>
> • A mechanism for bringing an individual or group that has wants and needs together with an individual or group that can satisfy those wants and needs

- A focus on understanding and serving the client, customer, or consumer

When looked at in these terms, marketing certainly is compatible with the approach, philosophy, and values of the nonprofit organization.

Thus marketing is at once a process and a set of tools, a function that can be used to enhance the effectiveness of an organization in fulfilling its mission to satisfy needs and wants. As such, marketing is a prime management responsibility of the executive.

The board has a limited but important role in marketing. A sound marketing program is wholly dependent on strong strategic planning—a clear definition of the purposes and programs and an enlightened vision for the organization—which is for the board to determine. The board also, as it does for all programs, oversees the marketing effort. And individual board members, where appropriate, can assist the executive and staff in their marketing efforts, especially when they have important contacts in the community.

It is up to the executive and staff, therefore, to identify for each of the organization's various constituencies or stakeholders what the needs and wants of that constituency are and how those needs and wants can best be met; then, using the best public relations tools available, promote the acceptance and use of the organization's programs designed to meet those needs. These measures also include more general steps to raise the public image of the organization as a whole.

For most nonprofit organizations, the executive and staff, in taking these first steps in the process, will identify the needs and wants of the following different kinds of constituencies or stakeholders:

- *Paying clients* (or customers). Schools and colleges have students who pay tuitions; museums and theaters have visitors and audiences who pay admissions; hospitals have patients whose care gets paid for or reimbursed.

- *Beneficiaries* (nonpaying clients). Community service organizations have the homeless, abused children, and many others.

- *Contractors*. Many organizations, especially community service organizations, live by government contracts and fees.

- *Donors*. Most nonprofit organizations depend on contributions to sustain and support the organization and its programs.

- *General public*. The public benefits from environmental, public policy advocacy, or charitable services that help the community as a whole.

The marketing process then turns to actions to meet those needs, reaching out to persuade, enlist, support, and convince. It employs the tools and techniques of public relations, including promotion and stewardship, "branding," printed materials, catalogues, newsletters, Web sites, e-mail, advertising, group meetings, conferences, events, volunteer efforts, gifts, and so on.

Marketing in this way can flourish, often being the essential element in the overall success of an organization.

Pitfalls

A cautionary footnote on marketing is offered by George Washington University Professor Amitai Etzioni (2002): "Debates continued over whether ethics should . . . be integrated into all [business school] classes. A member of . . . the marketing department mused that if the . . . policy were adopted, his department would have to close because much of what it was teaching constituted a form of dissembling, selling small items in large boxes, putting hot colors on packages because they encourage people to buy impulsively, and so forth."

Currently the term *marketing* refers to a philosophy, a discipline, or a buzz word getting a great deal of attention but meaning different things to different people. Some devout marketeers, calling for nonprofits to accept business marketing practices unreservedly, seem to overlook that many, possibly most, nonprofit organizations exist to provide public services and products—whether paid for or free—because there is no way business and the marketplace can sustain them. This is true in education, health, and culture.

Almost by definition, marketing is related to sales and selling—the "marketplace." It therefore has validity for nonprofit organizations in advancing their revenue-producing programs. For fund raising however—asking people to give, not buy, in support of public services—there is little or no place for marketing.

10

Fund Raising

Confusion often surrounds the responsibility for fund raising. Some board members believe that, because they are volunteers, it is not their job but the staff's to raise money to support programs. Some staff people, on the other hand, say they are involved in programs, and it is up to the board to raise the money.

Neither is right.

The job of raising contributed income is a central part of the partnership of board and staff. Neither can do it alone. In no other area of board and staff activity is the need so great for close and mutually supportive action of the Leadership Team.

The manner in which staffs and boards go about fund raising will be different for every organization. Fund raising will depend, first, on the type of organization—healthcare, cultural, education, community service, research, advocacy. Each organization will call into play different procedures, priorities, and tactics, depending on the relative importance of different sources—individuals, foundations, businesses, grantmaking organizations, or government agencies.

Kinds of Contributed Funds

In essence fund raising is a process of attracting contributed funds: donations, as distinct from earned revenues; tuitions; admissions; and fees for service. Contributed funds are of three kinds: those in *support of operations*—program and overhead expenses; those raised for *capital funds for buildings and endowments;* and *planned gifts*—a special kind of capital donation. The process and the challenge to the Leadership Team is a matter of sorting out the roles of the executive and staff and of the board in raising these three kinds of funds.

In addition to these process matters, Leadership Teams will constantly be concerned with the *size of development staff*, the *costs of fund raising,* and the *use of consultants* in fund raising.

Take each type of income one at a time.

Operational Funds

Start with managerial responsibilities in operational fund raising. The executive and development staff

- Keep the files—records, mailing lists, acknowledgment routines, renewal requests—that are requisite to any fund-raising process

- Prepare the *case* why people should support the organization and its programs—a core instrument in the whole process

- Research prospective supporters—foundations, corporations, major individual donors

- Manage the annual appeal—reaching out to members and regular contributors on the organization's own lists or to prospects by mass mailings to purchased or brokered lists

- Prepare proposals and correspondence

- Visit donors and prospects—whether as stewardship, cultivation, or for solicitation of a contribution

These functions are summarized in Exhibit 10.1, which allows the efforts of executive and staff to be scored. Apply a score of one

Exhibit 10.1. Staff Role in Fund Raising.

(Score 1–5)

1. **Files**—maintain records, mailing lists, renewals, acknowledgments   _____

2. **The case**—draft the case for why people should support the organization and its programs   _____

3. **Prospect research**—research individuals, foundations, corporations, government agencies   _____

4. **Annual appeal**—mount and manage   _____

5. **Proposals and correspondence**—prepare and follow up   _____

6. **Cultivation and solicitation visits**—set up, attend when appropriate   _____

7. **Initiative**—generate ideas, projects   _____

8. **Support board members**—motivate, encourage, stimulate, *thank*   _____

to five for each element, with five being the highest. A score of forty would be perfection. Low scores on any one element point to the need for improvement in managing the overall fund-raising role.

Turn then to the role of board members in raising operational funds, where every board member must be directly and personally involved. Boards cannot simply turn the job over to a committee or to staff. While in almost all of its other responsibilities board members deliberate, discuss, and decide matters, in fund raising they participate.

The board's fund-raising role starts with its responsibility for determining the organization's mission. The mission is particularly important to fund raising, as it helps make the *case* why people should support the organization. It's the central statement of the fund-raising appeal.

The board's overall responsibility to oversee performance also has special importance in fund raising because the board quite specifically approves the development program. The board's oversight of the fund-raising program is centered in the development committee, which has the key role not only in working closely with the staff on all aspects of fund raising but also, and especially, in stimulating and leading board members in fulfilling their share in the partnership.

Individual board members take an active part in specific fund-raising activities in the following ways:

- They contribute. Without exception, every member contributes personally and annually.

- They add names to the mailing list.

- They help identify and evaluate prospects. Board members know their peers among the individuals, corporations, and foundations most likely to contribute.

- They assist in cultivation of key prospects.

- They participate in annual appeals. Personal notes by board members on annual appeals will increase positive responses four- or fivefold.

- They are the best ones to engage in telephone appeals.

- They make introductions. Board members are often in the best position to help in this most critical and difficult step in approaching key corporate or foundation officials.

- They manage or assist in fund-raising events. This is a prime role for volunteer board members, especially when it relieves staff from being diverted from program duties.

- They write supporting letters. A board member's endorsement of a proposal to a corporation or foundation significantly enhances its chances.

- They write thank-you letters. A board member's word of appreciation for a grant is the first step in the next solicitation.

- They accompany staff or another board member on a solicitation. Their participation adds weight to the solicitation; it is also the best training exercise in learning to ask for gifts for the board member.

- Finally, board members can solicit a contribution— make the "ask."

Board members can be especially valuable in seeking grants from foundations, corporations, and government agencies. In securing the first introduction, board members can surmount the most difficult hurdle to overcome in a solicitation. A board member joining in a visit to a corporation, foundation, or government agency will significantly enhance the chances of success.

Not to be overlooked in all the foregoing activities, the assistance of the executive and staff to board members is immensely important to the fund-raising partnership. Staff can point the way, motivate, encourage, thank, even at times restrain the members. Inevitably staffs have to deal with the troublesome hazard of board members failing to do the things they promise to do and, being human, procrastinating.

Boards can be stimulated to greater involvement in their duties by scoring themselves in Exhibit 10.2 to assess their own participation. Apply a score of one to five for each element, with five being the highest. A score of eighty would be perfection. Fifty-five and above means the board is well engaged in fund raising. Below fifty-five, the board

Exhibit 10.2. Board Participation in Fund Raising.

(Score 1–5)

	self	board
1. Personal contributions.	_____	_____
2. Participation in strategic planning.	_____	_____
3. Review and endorse development plans.	_____	_____
4. Add names to the mailing list.	_____	_____
5. Help identify and evaluate prospects. • Individuals, foundations, corporations • Other grant-making nonprofits, government agencies	_____	_____
6. Share in cultivation of prospects.	_____	_____
7. Make introductions to key prospects.	_____	_____
8. Write notes on annual appeal letters.	_____	_____
9. Participate in telephone appeals.	_____	_____
10. Help manage fund-raising events.	_____	_____
11. Write supporting letters.	_____	_____
12. Write thank-you letters.	_____	_____
13. Accompany others in solicitation.	_____	_____
14. Ask for a contribution.	_____	_____
Also		
15. Actually do what you undertake to do.	_____	_____
16. Do not procrastinate.	_____	_____

may want to discuss or receive consultation or training in its appropriate role in fund raising.

Capital Funding for Buildings and Endowments

Attracting funds to pay for buildings or to build endowments takes donations of a different order of magnitude from funds to support programs and calls for different fund-raising ways and means—in promotion, cultivation, and solicitation. In particular, individuals—who are the principal donors in most capital fund raising—are called on to draw from their own capital assets, rather than their income, to make major, "stretch" donations.

Capital fund raising usually calls for a campaign, that is, a special effort that has its own organization, timeline, and goal. The key components of a capital campaign are three:

- *Readiness.* A careful evaluation of whether the organization is clear and agreed on its mission and its need for capital funds, has a strong cadre of supporters, and has a leadership fully committed.

- *Potential.* An assessment of the whether "the money is out there"; that is, whether the organization's support constituency is prepared to give such capital funds.

- A *campaign plan.* An organizational framework, a realistic timeline, and a budget.

Although strong staff involvement is a necessary part of any capital campaign, board leadership is of central importance, often difficult to pin down. Make no mistake: capital fund raising commands, as does no other activity in a nonprofit organization, the uncompromised commitment and exceptional effort of the Leadership Team—the board, the chair, the chief executive, and the development staff.

Planned Giving

Planned giving is a specialized, technical kind of long-term capital fund raising. *Planned gifts* are present commitments of donations that the recipient institution may not receive for a period of time and where the donors often receive lifetime incomes or benefits, beyond tax advantages, for themselves and beneficiaries. Planned giving programs usually involve major donations by friends of an organization who want to give more than they are able to do in an outright gift.

Because of these special aspects, planned giving programs are developed quite separately from those to solicit individuals in annual appeals or capital campaigns. As in those activities, it is important that the executive and staff provide the initiative, help identify prospects, and keep the records. However, because planned giving usually involves special relationships with affluent prospects, patient cultivation, and legal estate-planning arrangements, board members are central to the process.

Size of Development Staffs

The Leadership Team may be concerned with the size and shape of the fund-raising staff, not knowing how large a staff and what skills and experience are called for. The staff engaged in development range from the small community service organization that may rely on the executive alone to, at the other extreme, universities, hospitals, large cultural institutions, and national institutions where the chief executive usually has a director of development—even a vice president for development—with subordinates specializing in annual giving and memberships, corporate or foundation giving, or planned giving. Another question that often arises is whether public affairs should be subordinated to development or be a separate department.

There can be no rule of thumb to dictate the correct size of staff. Requirements will vary not only with the overall size of the organization and proportionately the size of the fund raising effort but also with the range of effort—sources of operational funds, capital campaign, planned giving.

Costs of Fund Raising

The costs of fund raising have to be a major concern of the Leadership Team both in terms of program oversight and because these costs often get public attention and special scrutiny by donors—foundations, corporations, United Ways, and even individuals.

The costs of raising money can be an elusive target to pin down. Assignment of costs to fund raising, to programs, to administration, or to public relations is by no means clear. Costs, too, can vary significantly with different types of organizations—education, healthcare, cultural, community services, research and advocacy—as well as with geographic location and with organizational size and maturity.

A simple assignment of cost per dollar raised, therefore, is usually misleading; the different forms of fund raising have widely different costs. Direct mass mail in an initial phase of donor acquisition, for example, can cost as much as $1.50 for each initial dollar raised (assuming a 1 percent return), and then go down to twenty cents for renewals (assuming a 50 percent return). These figures are in contrast to constituency annual giving or membership "dues" where, if volunteers are stuffing envelopes, the cost is little more than the postage.

Special benefit events are also expensive, costing as much as fifty cents for each dollar raised; but events have a public relations value as well as a fund raising one. Experts suggest that solicitations and proposals for corporate and foundation grants may average about twenty cents for each dollar raised.

Capital campaigns are a different story. Because the level of gifts is high, the effort is intense, and volunteers are involved, the costs can be as low as five or ten cents for each dollar raised. Planned giving capital fund raising, a long-term effort, is particularly hard to judge, but could come out at, say, twenty-five cents for each dollar raised.

The great variety in fund-raising costs for different kinds of organizations is illustrated in a selected list drawn from the *Chronicle of Philanthropy*'s "Philanthropy 400" (2002) (see Exhibit 10.3), showing fund-raising expenses as a percentage of total private support (contributions) and as a percentage of total income.

Using Consultants in Fund Raising

Although the use of consultants generally by nonprofit organizations is discussed in Chapter Sixteen, their frequent use in various aspects of fund raising deserves special attention.

Consultants can be of great assistance in guiding organizations in several different aspects of their development program:

- *Fund raising audits.* Nonprofit boards and executives constantly need to know whether the fund-raising program is in fact doing all it should and fulfilling its potential in attracting the resources needed to carry out the program. An outside professional consultant can undertake an objective, informed review of an entire development program, recommending helpful procedures, staffing, and board participation, and generally setting out a strategy for the program.

- *Mass direct mail appeals.* A major program to solicit donations by mass appeal to brokered and leased mailing lists—not to be confused with annual mail appeals to an organization's own mailing list—is highly specialized and technical; most organizations find it advantageous to retain professional assistance in managing the program.

- *Proposal writing.* Drafting proposals for foundation or corporate grants sometimes benefits from consulting assistance.

Exhibit 10.3. A Selection from the *Chronicle of Philanthropy's* "Philanthropy 400" Fund-Raising Expenses.

		Percentage of Private Support (contributions)	Percentage of Total Income
1	SALVATION ARMY	7.3	5.4
7	HARVARD UNIVERSITY	8.4	1.3
9	AMERICAN RED CROSS	16.4	4.0
10	METROPOLITAN MUSEUM OF ART	1.5	1.0
11	STANFORD UNIVERSITY	10.3	1.7
29	BOY SCOUTS OF AMERICA	15.4	6.1
30	GOODWILL INDUSTRIES INTERNAT'L	3.5	.5
49	MARCH OF DIMES BIRTH DEFECTS	18.3	16.9
51	U.S. FUND FOR UNICEF	11.1	10.6
53	NEW YORK COMMUNITY TRUST	.6	.6
68	UNITED JEWISH APPEAL	16.8	15.7
93	EASTER SEALS	28.3	6.5
96	ALZHEIMER'S ASSOCIATION	18.6	15.4
134	UNITED WAY OF NEW YORK CITY	18.8	1.
139	DISABLED AMERICAN VETERANS	30.3	25.0
179	PARALYZED VETERANS OF AMERICA	40.6	39.7
188	DIRECT RELIEF INTERNATIONAL	.4	.4
239	HUMANE SOCIETY OF THE U.S.	34.	31.
272	U.S. OLYMPIC COMMITTEE	32.4	17.4
318	NATIONAL WILDLIFE FEDERATION	22.	9.2
357	COMMUNITY FOUNDATION OF GREATER WASHINGTON	1.2	.9
358	AMNESTY INTERNATIONAL	13.4	12.7

Source: Chronicle of Philanthropy, 2002. Reprinted with permission.

- *Capital campaigns*. Professional consulting assistance is almost always essential in capital campaigns. Consultants can advise on the readiness to undertake a campaign—often by a development audit. They can provide a reliable assessment of the potential through constituency surveys (feasibility studies). And they can prepare comprehensive campaign plans including goals, case statements, procedures, and organization. In some cases they can manage the campaign, short of actually soliciting donations.

- *Planned giving*. Professional help is almost always called for in this highly technical aspect of fund raising. Moreover, in an exceptional role, consultants in planned giving can actually participate in negotiating gifts with prospects (though it is important that prospects also have their advisor involved in the negotiation).

- *Fund-raising events*. Independent management of fund-raising events—galas, luncheons, auctions, runs—is altogether appropriate and often labor-saving as well as effective.

- *Fund-raising accounting software*. Consultants can help with selection among dozens of software packages and with their installation and technical assistance during initial use.

- *General assistance*. Many organizations keep a fund-raising consultant on retainer, on hand for guidance in any and all aspects of the fund-raising effort.

Wholly different problems arise in retaining consultants actually to solicit contributions on behalf of the organization, principally by mass telephone appeals. Organizations should be wary of engaging fund raisers who will be representing the organization to the public yet have no direct connection with it or its mission.

Pitfalls

Responsibility

Although there are exceptions, responsible nonprofit organizations presumably do the fund raising themselves; they may hire a consultant to advise, but not to raise money for them; they themselves solicit support.

In the fund-raising profession, unlike the legal profession, it is unethical to pay fees, or salaries, or otherwise reward a fund raiser on a "commission basis" determined by the amount of money raised. In any event, with a consultant retained to raise money for an organization, the underlying charitable, philanthropic purpose of a contribution can get lost when the solicitation is driven by the monetary urge to extract a donation.

The Quick Fix

In the fund-raising world, the most common pitfalls are those of not understanding the fundamentals, or not recognizing the essential features of the process, and putting all the effort into only one source or one kind of fund raising. Many inexperienced board members, and even an occasional executive, harbor the illusion that if they could only get one or a few wealthy donors to underwrite the organization, they could avoid the burden of establishing a comprehensive fund-raising program.

Others say, "Let's go for an endowment and we won't have to worry about the annual budget deficit." It doesn't work. Big donations—individual, foundation, corporate—come from donors who have both the capability—the affluence—and an interest in the organization. One without the other is valueless. Major donations come only as the result of diligent cultivation of that interest, and that takes time and effort. A special hazard can arise in dealing with fund-raising events when emphasis on them distorts the whole development program.

Wrongful Allocation of a Donation

One specific and all-too-common pitfall is technically more a management action than a fund-raising one: no matter how tempting, an organization should never spend a designated contribution granted for a specific program or project on anything else.

The "Give, Get, or Get Off" Syndrome

Clearly every board member should make an annual personal contribution to the organization on whose board they serve. It is an act of commitment. Everyone is capable of giving something. And some grantmaking organizations, with good reason, will not make a donation unless there is 100 percent board giving.

But should every board member be called upon to give, or get others to give, a prescribed amount?

Some organizations find that board members will be stimulated into giving at a higher level than they otherwise would if a specific amount is set for all members. On the other hand, there are strong reasons against such a policy:

- It assumes a general equality in board members' capability to give and ability to attract contributions from others.

- Setting a figure presents a ceiling; people are inclined to accept a suggested amount.

- The policy is difficult to enforce. Throwing a member off for lack of making a major contribution cannot escape adverse feeling, and the inevitable exceptions and compromises can bring into question the board's consistency and the validity of the policy itself.

- Surely the basic esprit of a board is reduced when a monetary value is placed on membership.

Fund-Raising Events

Probably the most common misapprehension held by board members is the expectation that large amounts of money can be quickly and inexpensively raised through a fund-raising event. While board members can be especially helpful in this kind of "social fund-raising," such events can also engage the board's enthusiasm to a point of diverting attention from other important sources of funding support.

Ideas for fund-raising events are a dime a dozen, but the competition is staggering. Moreover, it must be understood that mounting events is labor intensive, with the work too often put upon a busy staff, taking them away from important program duties. A small net return after expenses is likely and is not worth the trouble, even when the public relations values are factored in. One keeps hearing of events earning vast sums for an organization; in fact, major financial success from fund-raising events usually comes only to high-profile charities that have built a tradition and strong body of regular attendees of their events.

The Development Officer

Donors like to give to their peers—board members or chief executive officers; they don't like to give to staff fund raisers. Board members therefore must accept that the development officer is not the frontline fund raiser. It is better to say that, unlike children, "A development officer should be heard, not seen." Development officers do the research, the preparation, draft the correspondence, lead the way, but the board-member partner in fund raising does the asking.

11

Enhancing Board Effectiveness

If, as should be beyond question, the effectiveness of the board is a key factor in the effectiveness of the whole organization, it follows that the board must make certain it is functioning properly; that is, fulfilling its responsibilities and maintaining its own organization and orderly procedures.

It is not possible to prescribe specific practices that characterize all effective boards against which to judge any single board's competence because such practices differ with organizations of different kinds, sizes, and purposes. However, effective boards will be deliberate and thorough in ensuring their own performance in two dimensions: fulfilling the five specific governance responsibilities discussed in the preceding chapters; and establishing and maintaining their own strong organization and procedures—the sixth responsibility of a board.

Although the effectiveness of a board in both of these dimensions will depend in large measure on the leadership of the chair, the executive will regularly be a positive force in helping the board perform well. Consultant Maureen Robinson (1998) says succinctly, "The more effort an executive makes to develop a strong board, the stronger the underlying relationship will be between the board and staff, and the more confidence and respect the board will have in the executive's work." And the more effective both will be.

Bylaws

The function of bylaws in the organization and procedures should be clearly understood. The institution's bylaws will set out the basic organizational structure but not the responsibilities of the board, nor the procedures by which the board operates. Like the Constitution, bylaws should not be rigid or too detailed. And boards should not be prisoners of their bylaws; unlike the legal Articles of Incorporation, the bylaws are there to reflect what the board wishes the organization to be, not to confine it; they can be amended.

Board Governance Responsibilities

A board must be quite deliberate in keeping under constant review just how well it performs with respect to each of the first five responsibilities it has, which were discussed in the introduction to Part Two and in Chapter Seven (for review, see Exhibit II.1).

The manner in which the executive assists the board in each of these responsibilities has been discussed in previous chapters. However there is one critical element—pervasive in all management and governance functions, and fundamental to the relationships within the Leadership Team—where the executive has a dominant position: it is the flow of information. To an almost exclusive extent, the executive controls the information the board needs to function and be effective. It behooves the executive, therefore, without exception, to be open and forthcoming with the flow of information the board needs to fulfill its responsibilities. Indeed, for the executive to keep away from the board any information relating to its activities is to court disaster.

This obligation, this mandate applies especially to unpleasant, unwelcome information, which it is often most tempting to withhold. Withholding any information can cause great strain between the board and the executive.

In sum, executives will regret it if they do not do everything in their power to make the board as strong as possible. They can help in many ways, starting with assisting in recruiting board members and continuing with helping in each aspect of board responsibilities and procedures. The executives must not be deluded into thinking that their position will be stronger, or easier, if their boards are weak, or to harbor the illusion that they can protect themselves by holding on to information. It just doesn't work that way.

For boards—and executives—to assess board performance in fulfilling governance responsibilities, Exhibit 11.1 provides an evaluation form. Apply a score of one to five for each element, with five being the highest. A score of sixty would be perfection. Forty and above means the board is doing fairly well. Below forty, the board may want to think seriously about how to improve its performance.

Board Organization and Procedures

All boards need to pay attention to the following aspects of organization and procedures: *board composition, member recruitment, officer selection and succession, committees, meetings,* and *self-evaluation.*

As with boards fulfilling their underlying responsibilities, so also can they be helped by the executive in their handling matters of organization and procedures.

Board Composition and Tenure

Composition is a matter of size and the tenure of membership. It involves not only the bylaws but also the personal qualities and skills of members.

In terms of size, unlike their corporate counterparts, whose boards are small and efficient, nonprofit boards, for several reasons, are usually more effective when they are fairly large. Numbers allow for diversity in age, race, and gender. Numbers permit a board to have members with direct knowledge and experience in program matters; members with professional skills—legal, accounting, fund raising, public relations and the like; and members with prestige in the community, who have access to funding sources. Especially,

Exhibit 11.1. Board Governance Responsibilities.

(Score 1–5)

1. **Mission**
   - To define the mission   _____
   - To participate in strategic planning: to review
     programs, purposes, priorities, and vision of the future   _____

2. **Chief executive**
   - To ensure selection and compensation   _____
   - To arrange regular performance evaluation   _____

3. **Finances**
   - To approve an annual budget   _____
   - To contract for an independent audit   _____
   - To control investment of funds   _____

4. **Program oversight and support**
   - To oversee and evaluate programs   _____
   - To support the staff   _____
   - To be an advocate in the community   _____

5. **Fund raising**
   - To contribute personally and annually   _____
   - To participate in fund raising   _____

numbers ensure that the views and needs of an organization's various constituencies—beneficiaries, sponsors, donors, community figures, associate organizations—can be understood and properly served.

Accordingly, nonprofit boards seeking to have a membership at once reflecting diversity, needed skills, and drawn from several constituencies usually find it necessary to have at least fifteen to twenty members. When membership runs to forty and more, it is hard to sustain interest and decision making becomes increasingly difficult.

Naturally the personal qualities of members, the "personalities" apart from skills, make a big difference. Part One, The Qualities of

Shared Leadership, especially Chapter Two, What an Executive Expects of the Board, reviews the needed qualities.

The question arises whether the executive should be a member of the board, with or without a vote. Most nonprofits find it highly desirable to have the executive a member, certainly attending all meetings except executive sessions. Unlike a business organization, however, the chief executive of a nonprofit organization should never be the chair.

As for whether the executive should have a vote on the board, except for large universities, hospitals, and museums, the executive is rarely a voting member. After all, the executive is not a volunteer and is hired, paid, and if necessary dismissed by the board. Although executives sometimes claim that the prestige of voting board membership assists them in fulfilling their responsibilities, that is hard to demonstrate; it won't make a good executive out of one falling short, nor will it add any authority to a good executive.

In reality boards don't vote very often; they seek consensus, and if the executive's vote is ever needed to make a majority, the board organization is probably in deeper trouble than the voting rights of the executive.

Organizations wishing to retain the involvement of more strong supporters than it can put on its board can sometimes form councils or advisory committees. But the trustee board holds the responsibility and actually governs.

Advisory councils must be carefully thought out. They must be given enough to do to prevent being meaningless but not so much as to interfere with the authority of the governing board. Members can be kept informed of organization affairs, attend meetings, perhaps meet together for briefings, but mostly be called on individually to make an important introduction.

Turning to tenure, boards can maintain vitality by limiting members' terms. Thus members can be elected to serve terms of two, three, or four years, with perhaps two successive terms permitted, but then required to take a year off before being eligible to return to the board. Valued members can thus be reengaged, while those not attending or participating can simply not be reelected. Staggered terms—not bringing up all members for reelection at the same time—achieve continuity.

In sum, boards will want to be quite deliberate in determining their own composition—the diversity, representation, and skills in their own makeup. The executive, familiar with the community and with the organization's needs, can help in reviewing the composition, identifying prospective members, and even recruiting board members.

Board Recruitment

Achieving and maintaining a strong governing board is a constant and challenging demand on the Leadership Team, especially the chair and executive. Too often the difficulties in recruiting strong members, and the role of the executive in the task, are underestimated.

Accordingly, for every nonprofit board and for its Leadership Team, recruiting new members deserves continued high priority. Every board member should feel a keen responsibility to keep the board membership strong.

Recruitment centers on finding candidates with an interest and a will to get immersed and participate. For boards of small community organizations, the problem involves scouring the community. For big national organizations, the choice is real and difficult: to go for the highly prestigious CEO, who can command support—if he or she will—or for the less prestigious individual, who will attend and work.

Boards that are quite deliberate in analyzing the current membership skills and strengths and what is missing can then go out and find the members they want.

Asking someone to join the board is itself a sensitive matter. It is awkward to invite someone to join unless assured the board will elect them. On the other hand, you don't want to put a name up for election to the board unless you have reason to believe the candidate is willing. It calls for a minuet: first an informal testing of the board, then of the prospect.

The actual invitation for a prestigious person to join the board can be as important as soliciting a major gift and should be treated similarly. Choose carefully the right person to do the asking: rarely the executive or a staff member, often the chair; always someone the candidate respects. Ask in person, preferably by a visit, rather than by phone or letter.

An important aspect of recruiting is to install a regular procedure for orientation of new members.

While weak executives may want weak boards they can dominate, strong executives want strong boards. Strong executives will take a direct interest in the whole recruitment procedure, starting with the identification of suitable prospective members, and ensuring they are properly asked to join.

Board Officers

Deciding what officers to have, establishing terms of office, and putting into place an election procedure should not present difficulties. But the importance of ensuring continued strong leadership—an orderly succession—can't be overstated.

Again, it is in the executive's interest to help the board in fulfilling its responsibility to ensure the continuity of strong board leadership.

Board Committees

In few other areas are the determinations of the Leadership Team—especially the chair and the executive—more important than in the organization and functioning of the board committees. Often the overall effectiveness of the board depends on useful committee work. Yet board committees are virtually helpless without executive and staff support. Conversely, with strong support from staff, committees can be important instruments in ensuring board leadership and thus the competent functioning of the organization.

Note, however, that, except in special circumstances, boards do not delegate to committees the board's responsibility to decide matters. Rather, committees are charged with focusing the board's attention on those things that need board attention and making constructive recommendations for board action. Committees can dig deeply into a subject for the board and report.

Remember that not every board member is well-informed on every subject. Some plead innocence in matters of finance, fund raising, or a program specialty, but they want to be responsible in their participation. They need therefore to be able to turn to respected colleagues who do understand and have explored the subject before the board. Committees, standing or ad hoc, can fulfill this purpose.

Committee structure will reflect the board's engagement with its governance responsibilities. Differing concepts are discussed in Chapter Fifteen. Some will have boards concentrate on identified strategic purposes and establish ad hoc committees to focus attention on them. In other models boards align committees to the board's governance role; that is, on finance, fund raising, oversight, and the board's own effectiveness. Still other, more traditional models, emphasizing the board's oversight role, favor a committee structure along the lines of staff functions and departments that need to be watched over.

Regardless of model, most boards have need for standing committees on finance and budget and on development and fund raising, whose functions are altogether clear, and, as discussed below under self-assessment, a governance or trustee committee. Other committees may be appropriate, such as for audits and personnel policies.

Boards can suffer from too much committee activity, risking on the one hand encroaching into management with too active committees or on the other hand too inactive committees, causing the full board to get enmeshed in matters a committee could better have sifted through.

A helpful procedure is for each committee to set out annually its plans and targets of achievement for the coming year. The exercise helps committees sharpen their purposes and sets up a basis for periodic evaluation.

Board Meetings

Good board meetings are the mark of strong boards. Several ingredients make for successful meetings, with good attendance and enthusiastic involvement in organizational activities.

Close cooperative planning by the chair and executive, along with strong chairmanship, can produce thoughtful agendas, well-prepared papers, outcome-driven discussions—in short, productive meetings. Special effort should be made to make meetings interesting by regularly introducing substantive program matters so that meetings don't get constantly bogged down in budgets, fund raising, and administration.

Nonprofit boards occasionally need executive, off-the-record sessions to permit completely open and frank discussions or to take up sensitive personnel matters relating to board members or staff. If board agendas always include an executive session item, it can be passed over if not needed and thus avoid any sense of crisis if unexpectedly called.

Self-Assessment of Organization and Procedures

If the board's own effectiveness is so important to the organization, why not have a standing committee to watch over the board's activities, the fulfillment of its responsibilities, and report regularly to the board with recommendations for improvement?

A governance committee, or committee on trustees, can usefully assume the role of a nominating committee, but its broader function is to keep all the operating procedures of the board under surveillance—its meetings, paperwork, committee activities, board-staff relations, planning procedures—anything that relates to board effectiveness. Oversight of conflict of interest would fall within the purview of such a committee. Overseeing the executive evaluation, discussed in Chapter Five, is also appropriate for the governance committee. See Resource B for sample terms of reference, or mandate, for such a governance committee.

The executive can constantly assist the board and its governance committee in self-assessment. Some organizations also find that professional counsel in the form of a skilled facilitator, can assist the self-evaluation process. See Resource C for a set of guiding principles in board self-assessment.

Exhibit 11.1 offered the board a way of evaluating its performance in fulfilling responsibilities. Exhibit 11.2 provides a way of scoring the board on organization and procedures. As before, give each item a score of one to five, with five being the highest. For board organization and procedures, a score of 130 is perfect. A score of seventy shows that the board is fairly well organized but should pay attention to areas of weakness.

Quite apart from responsibilities, organization, and procedures, there are *qualities* of general competence an effective board will want to address. Is the board in a contextual sense attuned to the culture and values of the organization it governs? Is it fully abreast of the educational, interpersonal, analytical, political, and strategic qualities that make for a fully effective board? Exhibit 11.3 allows the board to score itself on overall board competence. When scoring the board on competence, a score of thirty is perfect. Again, pay attention to any areas receiving low scores and seek to improve board functioning in that area.

Pitfalls

Board Composition

The problem of having a board responsive to constituent interests often leads to misunderstanding about the need to have "constituency representation" on the board. While board members are drawn from

Exhibit 11.2. Board Organization and Procedures.

(Score 1–5)

1. Composition
   - Size   _____
   - Diversity   _____
   - Program knowledge   _____
   - Community representation   _____
   - Skills (legal, accounting, public relations, fund raising)   _____
   - Prestige   _____

2. Recruitment of members
   - Tenure and rotation of members   _____
   - Identification of board needs   _____
   - Review and selection of candidates   _____
   - Persuasive invitations   _____
   - Orientation   _____
   - Nominating committee performance   _____

3. Officers
   - Positions and terms   _____
   - Selection   _____
   - Performance   _____

4. Committee structure
   - Number and roles   _____
   - Terms of reference   _____
   - Performance   _____
   - Executive committee (dominance, value)   _____

5. Meetings
   - Frequency, time, and place   _____
   - Agendas   _____
   - Papers   _____
   - Openness of discussion   _____
   - Interest   _____

6. Leadership
   - Board-staff relations   _____
   - Performance   _____

Exhibit 11.3. Board Competence.

(Score 1–5)

1. **Contextual**—the board understands and takes into account the culture, values, mission, and norms of the organization it governs. _____

2. **Educational**—the board takes the necessary steps to ensure that members are well informed about the organization, the programmatic substance involved, professionals working there, and the board's own roles, responsibilities, and performance. _____

3. **Interpersonal**—the board nurtures the development of its members as a group, attends to the board's collective welfare, and fosters a sense of cohesiveness and teamwork. _____

4. **Analytical**—the board recognizes complexities and subtleties in the issues it faces, and it draws upon multiple perspectives to dissect complex problems and to synthesize appropriate responses. _____

5. **Political**—the board accepts that one of its primary responsibilities is to develop and maintain healthy two-way communications and positive relationships with key constituencies. _____

6. **Strategic**—the board helps envision and shape the institutional direction and helps ensure a strategic approach to the organizational future. _____

different constituencies, they do not represent those interests on the board in a parliamentary sense. Decisions are not made by members speaking "on behalf of" and "reporting to" special interests, such as parents or teachers in a school, or nurses in a hospital, or donors to a community service organization. Nonprofit organizations are not democracies where interests and constituencies are "represented," and board members are not "delegates." Rather, board members serve the public and make decisions on the board in the overall interest of the organization, not as representatives of any sector.

A further complication arises if the concept of representation can carry with it the necessity of a board member consulting within the constituency on matters coming before the board and reporting back information that may fall within the board's range of confidentiality.

Board Officers—Treasurer

An unsuspected pitfall lurks in the title and position of treasurer. The election or appointment of a treasurer in any nonprofit organization in almost every case is a misfit, inescapably introducing confusion of governance and management responsibilities.

If the treasurer is a staff member, he or she answers to the chief executive in carrying out the financial operations. The title of business manager or chief financial officer (CFO) is more appropriate for staff than that of treasurer.

If the treasurer is a board member, it may mean or imply that an unpaid volunteer, outside the authority of the executive, has a responsibility for the management—not the oversight—of the finances of the organization, which in fact is the responsibility of the executive. The board's role is more fittingly met by a chair of the finance and budget committee, with responsibility to focus the board's attention on its appropriate oversight financial role.

If local laws require the board to have a treasurer, be sure the role is defined: if a board member, the responsibility is confined to oversight, not management; if a staff member, the officer answers to the chief executive whom the board holds responsible for the management of all matters, including financial.

Board Committees

Two kinds of committees can be controversial and present difficulties.

An executive committee can be useful, even essential, if its authority is confined to taking necessary actions between board meetings or when given authority to make decisions on a specific subject. However, when an executive committee makes decisions in place of the board, or reviews and virtually decides matters before they come to the board, the responsibility—and the interest—of board members are significantly diminished. Consultant Arthur Frantzreb (1996) puts it succinctly: "Executive committees which 'run' non-profit organization governing boards relegate all other members to second-class citizens. Second-class trustees should depart from 'first class' organizations."

In a word, the stronger the executive committee, the weaker the board is likely to be. Executives should not welcome strong executive committees.

Executive committees are justified in organizations that have such large boards that they cannot meet and govern effectively. In that case, board responsibilities must be delegated to an executive committee. However, in these circumstances the appropriate question turns on whether the organization is well served by having such a large board that it needs to have the executive committee. Would not the organization be better served by having a small, effective board and establishing a council or advisory committee to absorb the larger numbers?

Program committees—those set up to oversee the substantive program of an organization—run the risk of dominating program management. When such committees are established, the line between the board's governance oversight responsibility and executive's management must be carefully watched (see Chapter Four). Committee members must assiduously avoid giving direction to staff or allowing staff members to plead their case directly to the committee, thus going around the executive's direction. Though program committees are sometimes necessary and useful, unless carefully directed they can cause major trouble for an executive.

Board Meetings

The principal hazard in board meetings, other than misguided chairmanship, is boredom; it is important for chairs and executives to take the trouble to ensure that meetings are interesting and substantial—worth the attendance of busy members.

However, executive sessions, as a specific problem, can present difficulties and embarrassments if not handled deftly. As an example, the executive of an environmental organization threatened to resign if excluded from a board executive session the chair had called to discuss the executive's salary. The board gave in and as the resultant discussion was stilted, the session did not come to grips with important matters in the relationship of the executive to the board and the organization suffered.

12

Administrative Activities

Administration, a prime responsibility of the executive, includes the management activities in support of substantive programs. Other than general oversight, the board and individual board members normally have little to do with administration.

Arbitrarily, with financial management considered a separate subject, administration can be seen as composed of three areas: human resources; offices, facilities, procurements; and related or unrelated business activities.

Human Resources

The executive alone hires, compensates, directs, and evaluates all the staff. If necessary, the executive dismisses a staff member. The executive keeps full records on all personnel.

A list of the elements of managing human resources includes at least the following:

- Program planning and staffing patterns

- Job descriptions

- Hiring process

- Orientation and training

- Compensation

- Health and other benefits

- Supervision, evaluation

- Staff development

Many nonprofit organizations are heavily dependent on volunteers to provide mission-fulfilling services. Recruiting, training, motivating, and directing volunteers can then be an additional major matter in the administration of human resources, involving many of the same elements as for hired personnel.

In its approval of the budget, the board will have an impact on personnel matters. In addition, as a governance matter the board has responsibility for the personnel policies of an organization. Personnel policies in the normal course will cover most of the foregoing management elements as well as the following:

- Salary scales and bonuses

- Health and other benefits plans

- Discipline processes and dismissals

- Grievance procedures

- Compliance with the laws

However, as discussed in Chapter Five, the board leaves to the executive the hiring of all staff personnel, their direction, performance evaluation, compensation, and contract tenure.

Offices, Facilities, Procurements

An organization must be housed in an office or a building or several buildings in different locations. The board expects the executive to handle these matters, albeit under the watchful eye and with the possible assistance of the board, for such matters can be highly influential in the performance or the public image of the organization, with which the board has a vital interest.

More routine in the executive's responsibilities are the functioning facilities, appliances, and vehicles necessary in the operations and administration of the institution.

Related and Unrelated Business Activities

Many nonprofit organizations derive income from merchandise sales, gift shops, rental properties, lotteries, and auctions. Whether they are directly program-related, unrelated, or quasi-related, they need to be managed. They can form a major administrative responsibility left to the executive with the board's oversight.

Such activities, almost by definition, operate exactly like a business and will therefore be managed along businesslike, profit-making, and marketing lines, employing business models and practices.

Pitfalls

Conflicts of interest are a constant hazard in administration to be guarded against by both the executive and the board. Contractual services entered into with a person or company where a board or staff member has a beneficial interest is, in most cases, wholly inappropriate if not unethical, and certainly has to be fully disclosed.

Nepotism is rarely acceptable.

Part III

The Special Challenges
of Shared Leadership

Nonprofit leadership teams face many challenges and hazards, some of which deserve special attention.

These challenges cross over delineations of governance and management and move the Leadership Team into untried areas that will tax their competence and their need for mutual understanding and cooperation.

The following selection of challenges is discussed in the chapters of Part Three:

- Program Evaluation (Chapter Thirteen)

- Information and Communications Technologies (Chapter Fourteen)

- Exploring Different Governance and Management Concepts (including *venture philanthropy*, *capacity building*, *social enterprise*, and the *policy governance model*) (Chapter Fifteen)

- Using Consultants (Chapter Sixteen)

- Special Challenges Facing the Leadership Team (Chapter Seventeen)

- Accountability (Chapter Eighteen)

13

Program Evaluation

Much attention is being given to program evaluation in non-profit organizations—the assessment of effectiveness of programs and services.* And with good reason. Every organization needs to know how well it is fulfilling its mission. Board members, executives, donors, associated organizations, the public—all are concerned with performance and how it can be reliably evaluated and such an evaluation made known.

Books and handbooks are available on all aspects of the subject. Conferences and workshops are held. Some organizations and associations are dedicated exclusively to defining and developing procedures and providing evaluation services.

The importance of the subject for boards and executives is not in question, nor is the complexity of the subject. The significant questions to be clear on are these: *Why evaluate? Who does the evaluation? What to evaluate?* and *How to balance effectiveness with efficiency?*

---

*The term *program evaluation* is used rather than *performance evaluation* to ensure that there is no confusion or misunderstanding that the purpose of the evaluation is to learn about how a program is doing rather than whether the right people are doing an adequate job.

Why Evaluate

It is reasonable to separate three different aspects concerning planning the mission and programs of any organization:

- Identifying the community or national needs the organization exists to meet

- Providing the programs to meet those needs

- Evaluating the programs to determine whether the organization is fulfilling its mission and the programs are meeting the needs

The first two aspects are clearly a function of strategic planning, in which an organization determines deliberately why it exists, what it is going to do, and how it is going to do it. The third aspect, however, is quite different. An organization's leaders want and need to know reliably, "How are we doing—are the programs actually meeting the needs?"

There are many reasons, therefore, for nonprofit leaders to engage in program evaluation, starting with a board's and the executive's need to have a basis for judging whether the organization is truly fulfilling its purposes. A business can rely on sales, profits, and market share as readily available indicators of performance. Nonprofits, with no less a need to assess the worthiness of their organizations, are pressed to find other means of assessment. How do colleges and schools know they are really educating their students? How are hospitals assured they are providing all that is expected in the case of the sick, or museums that they are fulfilling their cultural contributions to the community?

Without evaluations, a board has a limited basis for fulfilling its other major responsibilities, particularly its oversight role. For both board and executive, a thorough evaluation can make convincing the appeal for supporting funds. Most important, boards and staffs can learn much from evaluations and raise the level of their own performance.

Evaluations may also be prompted by the need to satisfy funders and supporters—foundations, corporations, wealthy individuals, even members. They all want to know if their money is being put to good use.

Boards and executives therefore underestimate at their peril the importance of program evaluation. Allison Fine (1997), founder of Innovation Network (InnoNet), a nonprofit organization providing evaluation services, makes the point strongly: "Rather than rely on facts to chart their progress, nonprofit organizations continue to hide behind anecdotes and faith. And despite much talk over the last several years about the need for charities to be 'accountable,' the fact remains that most nonprofit groups don't know if they are producing positive results." She goes on to say, "Charities and grant makers both need to understand that evaluations are not extraneous exercises but central elements in planning and improvement of programs."

At the heart of evaluation is the recognition that program evaluation is not simply a matter of measuring outcomes. For nonprofit organizations performing or funding public services, assessing effectiveness raises the complex technicality of "social impact" and "return on investment" of programs and activities. It seeks to answer the question of what difference the programs actually make in the community. Political scientist David Campbell (2002) describes the dilemma:

> Leaders of nonprofit organizations face a particular bind in responding to demands for results-based accountability. If they focus only on the project-level outcomes over which they have the most control or for which indicators are readily available, they risk default on the larger question of accountability to publicly valued goals. On the other hand, if they try to demonstrate the impact of

their particular projects on community-wide outcomes, they risk taking credit inappropriately or shouldering the blame for indicators beyond their control.

Who Does the Evaluation

There are essentially two ways of performing program evaluations: they can be done internally or by an outsider.

If done internally, evaluation can be carried out by the staff, by a board committee, or by some combination of board, staff, clients, donors, and others who have an interest—that is, constituencies, or stakeholders. Internal evaluations have some advantages: staffs are the repository of most of the information needed; internal evaluation can be less expensive; and, particularly, insider evaluations can enhance the staff's ability to analyze their own performance and gain from it.

The trouble is, however, that internal evaluations can be highly diversionary of staff time, and, more important, can raise serious questions of objectivity, especially for staff participants. After all, evaluations inevitably are seen in large measure as assessments of the staff's own performance. No matter how fair-minded executives and staffs are, they are involved personally and cannot be detached and objective.

Outsider evaluations, while inevitably more expensive, have several advantages. Outside evaluators bring to the task well-honed professional evaluation skills and familiarity with the experience of similar institutions. You can be reasonably assured the assessment is thorough. Objectivity, too, can be expected, although even here the objectivity of an outsider is sometimes questioned: consultants may be thought to pull their punches in order not to displease a client they want to serve again. Moreover, outside evaluators can bring their own biases, posing their own questions to fit their own answers.

Think carefully about who should do the evaluation, but do it.

What to Evaluate

Some basic principles on what to evaluate and other aspects of the process of program evaluation, whether done internally or with an outsider, can be identified—all involving the board, the executive, and staff:

1. Requisite to successful program evaluation is a clear and comprehensive statement of the mission—the organization's purposes, programs, priorities. The object of the evaluation then is to assess how well the organization is fulfilling the mission. Because a clear and agreed-upon mission can usually emerge only through strategic planning, the two processes are closely intertwined.

2. At the heart of effective program evaluation, and one of its biggest hurdles, is the establishment of criteria, the measures by which judgments can be made about the organization's fulfillment of its mission. While many of the criteria can be quantified—the obvious financial figures, numbers of service recipients, and so on—much of the assessment of effectiveness will call for qualitative, nonquantifiable, subjective measures of success or imaginatively devised quantifications to apply to qualitative assessments.

Devising these criteria is what makes evaluations extremely difficult but by the same token especially important. What is involved here may be systematic "exit interviews" of patients or clients, or surveys of students over years after graduation. As is often said:

> Not everything that counts can be counted. Not everything that is important is measurable. It is better to be roughly right than precisely wrong.

The important point here is that the board, the executive, and any assisting consultant should agree on the criteria to be used, and what evidence will be convincing, in judging how effective a program is.

3. The process of program evaluation essentially involves a number of quite specific elements:

a. Careful planning of each step of the process.

b. Deliberate determination of the participants—board members, staff, service recipients, funders, observers, professional advisors.

c. Devising the right questions—a crucial and taxing task. Questions must address not only whether the organization is fulfilling its mission but also how well it is meeting the needs of the community. Boards can help enormously in framing these questions.

d. Comprehensive data collection—interviews, surveys, focus groups.

e. Constructive, objective analysis and assessment based on comprehensive, thoughtful criteria.

f. A useful report.

The board's governance role calls on it not only to ensure that the organization and its programs are regularly and properly evaluated to accord with the organization's mission and its directives but also to determine and oversee the process. Thus, consultant Peter Szanton (1998) states, "No matter how well chosen the evaluator and how clear the statement of objectives, the evaluation will often prove unsatisfactory unless a group of board members, together with the chief executive, approves the design, budget, and schedule of the study at the outset, and monitors its progress thereafter.

"One of the board's standing committees might assume that role, but an ad hoc committee formed specially for the purpose is generally preferred."

Reduced to the simplest terms, in evaluating programs, organizations—boards and executives—need to be clear and explicit on what they exist to do, whom they serve, and how well they do it. They also need to keep constantly in the forefront that the fundamental purpose of program evaluation is to improve the organization, not to break it down.

How to Balance Effectiveness and Efficiency

The matter of program evaluation inevitably brings to the forefront the distinction between efficiency and effectiveness. Efficiency relates to money-saving, labor-saving, time-saving—as in "business efficiency" and "cost efficiency." Effectiveness is a matter of maximum, or at least optimum, fulfillment of purpose. Peter Frumkin (2001) of Harvard's Kennedy School of Government states, "To be successful in the future, nonprofit managers will need to move the performance conversation consciously away from narrow process measures of efficiency to broader measures of program outcomes and impact, where nonprofits have some distinctive advantages."

Although grantmakers and individual donors often look for effectiveness in terms of the ratio of administrative costs to overall expenses, that path is full of brambles. Frumkin goes on to say, "Given the difficulty in sorting out differences in program effectiveness, many of the nonprofits have gravitated to the simple ratio of administrative to total expenses as an understandable and marketable benchmark for performance that can be trumpeted in fundraising appeals."

Board members and donors therefore need to be wary of making hasty judgments of performance by simplistic measures of administrative and fund-raising costs against money presumed allocated to program. Fund-raising costs are discussed in Chapter Ten. Similarly, administrative costs are by no means clearly defined and will be highly variable with the different charitable activities of education, healthcare, cultural activities, and community services. Nor can it be assumed that all other expenses can be tallied up as program costs.

Pitfalls

Two common hazards of program evaluation should be recognized. First, positive steps need to be taken to avoid having the staff either too dominant or, conversely, find themselves threatened—seeing the process as questioning their personal performance. The goal must be to achieve a balance in testing effectiveness while bringing about improvement.

Second, it is difficult but always important to ensure strict objectivity and concentration on the fundamental programmatic purposes the organization exists to provide. This problem can be especially troublesome when an assessment is triggered by a funder whom an organization quite naturally hopes to impress. In this regard, Professor Richard Chait (1993) has a useful caution: "Unlike their counterparts in for-profit corporations, most trustees do not see clearly what ultimately matters for nonprofit organizations and how institutional performance should be measured. As a result, many board members see little choice but to focus on more familiar issues such as short-term management, especially financial performance, where they can readily chart progress. If, however, boards monitor only what they can measure, they then will rush headlong into administrative operations."

Other pitfalls associated with program evaluation are predictable:

- Because the task is arduous for the board and somewhat unwelcome for the executive and staff, evaluations are deferred or avoided.

- Unplanned, underestimated, and haphazard program evaluations can be harmful, introducing disagreements and controversy without constructive solutions.

- Boards that defer to staff the articulation of key questions, or delegate program evaluation to a committee or several committees, fail to fulfill an important responsibility and find illusory satisfaction in a job not properly done.

- Finally, Allison Fine notes, "The mistake too many groups make is to collect too much data. This is an exhausting process and when groups try to bite off too much—for instance trying to measure outcomes for every service—they wind up not completing the job. . . . Be strategic, keeping the questions to a minimum, focusing only on what you really need to know" (personal correspondence, 2000).

14

Information and
Communications Technologies

The information and communications technologies (ICTs) arising from the marvelous mechanism of the computer are having and will continue to have a profound, almost overwhelming effect on the way we deal with information and knowledge and the way we communicate with each other. Not surprisingly, the impact alters organizational relationships and touches fundamental values and behaviors in nonprofit institutions.

In essence, if knowledge is what one knows, or what is known, the technologies allow organizations to gather, sort, store, search, share, and distribute information, which vastly enhances what one can at any time know, transmit instantaneously to others, and use effectively in performing the functions related to management and governance.

Clearly the effective application of the technologies throughout the organization is a prime responsibility of the executive—the impact is felt in all the management functions. But governance functions will also be altered—board members cannot escape. In particular, the board's oversight role makes it a party to the effective manner in which the executive handles the technologies.

The task then is to get a clear picture of a big, confused, but very important dimension of governance and management facing the Leadership Team and see how it can be dealt with.

When the computer first came into our lives, it introduced one unexpected but critical demand: it forced organizations to undertake grueling, exasperating, but altogether rewarding efforts to review, self-analyze, and articulate with clarity and precision exactly what they were up to and where they wanted to go before the computer could ever be instructed to help. As a result, organizations must now undertake a detailed, demanding, introspective analysis of their information and communications needs in order to put the technologies to work effectively.

The question here then is simply this: What of the complex and pervasive opportunities and problems arising from the information and communications technologies need board members and executives of nonprofit organizations understand and deal with?

Surely, it is not just a matter of explaining the endless technical details of this new dimension. It can be assumed that many, perhaps most, nonprofit board members use the Internet, but they are likely not intimately familiar with the nature and use of the whole range of information and communications tools. Even if they have some familiarity with the ICT tools, they probably have not thought through the ICT tools in relation to specific governance and management functions.

Instead, at the constant risk of oversimplification, this chapter will identify the key tools arising from the ICTs that can be helpful in the operations of nonprofits and then seek to show how these tools can be applied most productively to the management and governance of organizations. Keep it simple. But not too simple. And most of all, be clear and precise.

At the outset, the Leadership Team must realize that the technologies derived from the computer have caused unforeseen but profound changes in the organizational culture, including shifts in roles, relationships, work styles, and power structures. Daryl Nardick (2002) of Conseq Associates, consultants who "help organizations manage the unintended consequences of IT changes," calls these changes the "human side of technology."

The following are some examples of the impacts board members and executives may need to watch for in planning the application of ICTs to their governance and management:

- How has the Internet changed the organization? Have peoples' interactions changed? If so, how? For example, does e-mail sometimes stimulate too-hasty judgments?

- Is there an unhealthy factor in the total concentration on the computer, as we stay put all day long without moving to manage and communicate?

- Are we losing control of time? Managing e-mail in and out can be totally absorbing. Many now complain, "I don't have time to read."

- Is life becoming depersonalized? Workers don't have to meet with their bosses, they e-mail them and get their replies. Researchers interact on-line. We don't have to go to the library, we go to the Internet. Why go to the store when you can get it without moving?

- Is there a generational bias? Those who grew up with the technologies may have an advantage over those who have had to learn—often with difficulty. Elder coworkers, not technology adept, can be left behind or out.

- Do the tech masters have all the power when it comes to ICT decision making? Knowledge is power. Many organizations leave ICT planning to those who most understand the technology.

An important lesson therefore emerges for the Leadership Team: in planning ICT changes, you cannot anticipate all the unintended consequences. However, you can reduce their impact if you are sure to include users, not just the experts, in the planning. Technicians can get absorbed in their hardware; users ask themselves, "Will this help me do my job better?"

Accordingly, board members and executives can start by being clear on the specific tools the technologies make available. They then look for the applications—how the various tools relate and apply to the specific operations and the various functions of management and governance.

At the outset, however, the big and complex field of technologies can be circumscribed. For the purpose of identifying just those key tools that are going to enhance the management and governance operations, it is necessary to exclude and not dwell on those general computer-generated tools that are so pervasive they apply to all operations and therefore do not have specific application to management and governance tasks. In this category would fall such everyday computer uses as:

- Word processing programs

- Spreadsheet programs

- Desktop publishing

- Presentation programs

- Personal programs for Internet access, calendars, date books, tasks, and so on

The basic ICT tools that do have a direct and specific application to the management and governance functions can be reduced to ten: four information and six communications tools. Admittedly arbitrary and by no means discrete, they are listed here and described summarily in the ensuing paragraphs.*

*The discussion on information tools is drawn principally from Enzer, M., *Matisse's Glossary of Internet Terms* (2000). Also note that although a database can be considered a single tool, for the purpose of this discussion it is seen as a collection of separate tools to accord with several different uses.

Information Tools

1. Database records and files

2. Database program information

3. Database name lists

4. Special functional programs

Communications Tools

1. E-mail

2. Web site

3. Internet research

4. Intranet

5. Widespread information distribution

6. Information gathering

The Information Tools

1. *Database records and files.* A body of official or nonofficial records and files—formal or informal—kept on the computer, largely replacing hard copies; readily available for authorized retrieval, reproduction, or communication; information organized by subject, source, or date; used in programs and operations. Examples are client records, vendor files, earned-income fees, contracts, sales, personnel records.

2. *Database program information.* Documents and texts filed in the computer for authorized retrieval, reproduction, communication, or discard. Examples are program designs, manuals, annual reports, "intellectual property" materials.

3. *Database name lists.* Lists of names stored in the computer in predetermined categories, capable of regular updating and retrievable for mailings. Examples are members, board and former board members, staff, constituencies, newsletter mailing lists.

4. *Special functional programs.* A myriad of computer programs specially designed for specific uses. Examples are institutionally

devised spreadsheets and financial forms, fund raising recording forms, operational case records.

The Communications Tools

1. *E-mail (electronic communication)*. Messages, usually text, sent via an Internet server from one person to another or automatically to a number of addressees (see widespread information distribution, below).

2. *Web site*. A home page on the World Wide Web (www—the universe of Internet networks, or computer facilities) that transmits text, graphics, and sound files, including hypertext (linking to other documents), that make it possible for a business, organization, or person to present their own facts, public relations material, or cat-alogue of merchandise for direct sale.

In simpler terms, Web site technology permits a particular type of Internet communication that allows information to be posted on the World Wide Web—you might say, the "electronic bulletin board"—available to all others on the Internet.

Web sites can vary significantly in size and complexity, with costs of developing and maintaining them mounting steeply when features are added, turning a Web site from a passive communication to one that will register responses ("hits") or provide collection capability, through credit cards or Internet-based services (such as PayPal or groundspring.org), for merchandise sales or for contributions.

3. *Internet research*. The capability through computer commu-nications to search out and retrieve information and documenta-tion on almost any subject, person, or organization.

4. *Intranet*. A private computer network for communication with-in a company or organization, including Web sites for internal use.

5. *Widespread information distribution*. The capability of distributing materials simultaneously to multiple, including massive, list recipients.

6. *Information gathering*. The capability of using computer com-munication to receive survey responses to questionnaires.

These tools are by no means mutually exclusive; rather, they can be effectively combined to serve multiple purposes.

For example, schools have Web sites that post information available to anyone interested in learning about the school. In addition, the school Web site will have a major intranet dimension available on a highly restricted basis for students, faculty, and parents, setting out, among other things, each student's academic profile, weekly schedule, assignments, extracurricular activities, pictures of all classmates, and, on an even more restricted basis, grades.

Another example shows the use of a special form—an institutionally designed functional information tool. Strive, a national organization of twenty affiliates providing job training and employment assistance for the willing but hard-to-employ, has designed a computer program that records ongoing case management information concerning employment for all clients in the system.

Application of the Technology Tools

Turn then to the several functions to which each of the foregoing ICT tools can be applied. These are the six management functions and the six governance functions described in Part Two:

Management Functions

1. Program direction
2. Promotion, public relations, and marketing
3. Fund raising
4. Financial management
5. Administration
   a. Human resources
   b. Office, facilities, and procurement
   c. Related business activities
6. Board support

Governance Functions

1. Hire executive

2. Mission and vision

3. Finance
   a. Budget
   b. Audit
   c. Investment

4. Oversight and support

5. Fund raising

6. Board effectiveness

Clearly all management functions can make extensive use of all the new information and communications tools, although in different ways and to different degrees for each kind of organization— educational, cultural, healthcare, community service. Today's executive must be well versed in the new technologies.

To a lesser degree, but still important, the information and communications technologies are helpful to boards in fulfilling their governance role.

The applications of the several tools to management and governance are summarized in the following paragraphs. A matrix chart is offered in the following section so that each organization may think through its own management and governance information and communications demands. Use of the matrix chart is described following the discussion of applications.

Applications to Management Functions

1. *Application to program direction.* Information tools, especially records of clients, patients, and beneficiaries, will be important to the program direction of most organizations regardless of mission. The special forms information tool provides a signal opportunity

for designing case management applications to enhance program direction.

Although larger institutions will count on e-mail for internal communication about program direction, for the most part ICTs will probably be less useful in program direction except where the programs directly involve research.

2. *Application to promotion, public relations, and marketing.* Records and list databases are essential information tools for marketing and public relations.

Web sites and information distribution are fundamental communications tools for marketing and public relations.

3. *Application to fund raising.* As Chapter Ten suggests, the new tools are all critical in every aspect of the fund-raising function.

Computer-based contribution records have virtually replaced hard-copy files. List databases of memberships, contributors, and prospects are absolutely essential to cultivation, appeals, solicitations, and stewardship. Computer program tools that develop special forms are used extensively in handling the fund-raising complexities of such technical matters as planned giving. Without advanced computer databasing, direct mass mail appeals—those targeting potential new donors using purchased or exchanged lists, in contrast to constituency mail appeals directed toward those on the organization's own mailing list—would not be possible.

On the communications side, Web sites, quite aside from their important use to fund raising of promoting the organization and its programs, have become extremely valuable as a medium to attract the interest of and solicit potential contributors.

Although cultivation and solicitation will always depend principally on personal contacts, in fund raising for major gifts—large donations and grants from individuals, business companies, and foundations—ICTs can be helpful on a selective basis. The Internet can be a useful additional research resource in identifying and evaluating new prospects. Web sites can provide readily available information on a wide range of prospective contributors.

An important parenthetical note is this: as nonprofit organizations move headlong into the world of new communications and information technologies, the field of fund raising using the Internet, called "e-philanthropy," needs standards and ethical guidance. The board must be the guardian of holding to the standards. The nonprofit ePhilanthropyFoundation.Org has prepared a code of ethics for on-line fund raising, including standards for donor privacy, security of on-line transactions, disclosure of all the organizations involved in handling on-line gifts, and resolution of complaints (see Resource D).

4. *Application to financial management.* The information technologies and computer manipulation of financial records have revolutionized the management of finances in every aspect—accounting, budgets, audits, investments, and financial reports.

5. *Application to administration.* To a lesser extent but still impressive, new technologies used in the management of human resources and in the controls over office, facilities, and especially procurements have made for enormous efficiencies.

The application of information and communications tools to unrelated business activities will depend on the type and size of the activity, but here the uses will be comparable to those found in business enterprises.

6. *Application to board support.* Management's use of information and communications tools in fulfilling its responsibility to support the board will relate directly to the use the board itself makes of the tools in its governance functions; management will not have any separate use in this respect.

Applications to Governance Functions

The several information and communications technology tools identified offer no special opportunities for the board independently fulfilling its six governance responsibilities, except where the board uses intranet—e-mail and "private" Web sites—to improve its own effectiveness by better internal communications.

The board will of course be using the products of these tools and be deeply involved with them in its oversight of all management functions, which themselves will be making extensive use of ICTs. Especially in its partnership role with the staff on fund raising, the board will be heavily involved with the new information and communications tools.

Using the Chart

The matrix chart, Exhibit 14.1, challenges each organization to analyze its information and communications needs and see how the several new ICT tools can be applied to its management and governance functions. The chart suggests assigning values—A for major dependence; B for major use; C for moderate use; D for minor use; and E for no use—in considering the application of each tool to each of the management and governance functions.

The chart is not designed for use by a computer or information or communications specialist but instead should be an analytical device for board members and staff to think through the organization's management and governance functions, the better to determine and define just which tools are right for each function, what applications can fit the management and governance or their organization.

Ultimately the impact on philanthropy of the new communications technology, especially on fund raising, will depend on how widespread and how rapidly people turn to the Internet and how completely it will replace traditional communications for the national population as a whole and for different segments—the young and the elderly; the affluent and the less affluent. One thing, however, seems certain: the importance of personal contacts in the operations of nonprofit organizations, especially in fund raising, can never be replaced by improvement and speed in handling information and communication.

Exhibit 14.1. Matrix Chart: Applying ICTs to Management and Governance.

	Information Tools			
	Records	Information database	List database	Special Forms
Management Functions				
1. Program direction				
2. Marketing/ PR				
3. Fund raising—staff				
4. Finance				
5. Administration				
(a) Human resources				
(b) Office/Facilities				
(c) Related business				
6. Board support				
Governance Functions				
1. Hire executive				
2. Mission				
3. Finances				
(a) Budget				
(b) Audit				
(c) Investment				
4. Oversight/Support				
5. Fund raising—board				
6. Board effectiveness				

Rating Scale: A = Major Dependence; B = Major Use; C = Moderate Use; D = Minor Use; E = No Use.

Communication Tools

E-mail	Web sites	Research	Intranet	Information distribution	Information gathering

Rating Scale: A = Major Dependence; B = Major Use; C = Moderate Use; D = Minor Use; E = No Use.

Pitfalls

One underlying misunderstanding of the information and communications technologies can arise, as simply expressed by Colin Moffet (2002) of Technology Works for Good, who warns, "The idea that every dollar a nonprofit spends on technology results in increased productivity is a myth. In this digitally crazed world, many have fallen under the illusion that all technology is good technology. . . . If you can plug it in, it must be able to help you do something good. The truth is that technology is just a tool—nothing more, nothing less."

> *In order to capitalize on the promise of technology, the tool has to fit the job.*

Another pitfall relates to a topic discussed earlier in this chapter, unintended consequences. Boards and executives must be vigilant in guarding against the dominance of tech-minded colleagues and be sure to involve users, not just technology experts, in all technology planning.

In a different direction, with access to information so universal and available, boards can be sorely tempted to fall into the other trap: using the new tool that has fallen in their lap to micromanage, meddling too intrusively into management's role.

15

Exploring Different Governance and Management Concepts

This chapter discusses the following governance and management concepts:

- Venture philanthropy

- Capacity building

- Social enterprise

- Policy Governance model

Nonprofit leaders—boards and executives—need to know about special concepts, some of them new, for philanthropy, governance, and management that may significantly affect how they go about their responsibilities. While the directions may be controversial, they also get a lot of attention and may present timely opportunities; they should not be ignored.

Venture Philanthropy

Since it came on the scene only in the last decade, the concept of venture philanthropy has been variously defined and described. The Edna McConnell Clark Foundation, as reported in *Venture Philanthropy 2001*, points out the following: "The term *venture philanthropy* has lacked definition from the beginning, and it seems only to be getting more confusing. An overly precise-sounding lexicon appears to be masking an enormous degree of ambiguity and need for learning. This has resulted in a great degree of uncertainty as to what comprises the field."*

This said, it seems reasonable that venture philanthropy can be seen as the application in the nonprofit sector of certain practices used in investing by business venture capitalists: notably, provision of both major cash funding and strategic management expertise; a long-term (four- to six-year) outlook; an intense, hands-on managing partner relationship with the receiving organization; a demand for measurement and strict accountability for outcomes and results; and an exit strategy.

The venture philanthropy concept has been introduced and promoted mostly by the entrepreneurs of dot-com technologies. As a concept, venture philanthropy is associated with much the same elements as are in capacity building and social enterprise, described below, that focus on organizational infrastructure and social purpose, including poising organizations for major growth and strengthened leadership.

Some philanthropic ventures have already achieved successes. For example, Coastal Enterprise in Wiscasset, Maine, has a mission "to help people and communities, especially those with low incomes, reach an equitable standard of living, working and learning in harmony with the natural environment." In its 2002 Annual Report it claimed, with eight branch offices, seventy-nine employees, and twenty-three AmeriCorps participants, to have participated in more than $300 million worth of economic development financing to twelve hundred businesses, social services, and housing projects; created or sustained some eleven thousand jobs; and counseled more than ten thousand small businesses.

*This and other quotations drawn from Morino Institute, *Venture Philanthropy 2001: The Changing Landscapes* are copyright © 2001 by the Morino Institute and prepared for the Morino Institute and Venture Philanthropy Partners by Community Wealth Ventures, Inc.

Another example (2001) is Venture Philanthropy Partners of Washington, D.C., a nonprofit philanthropic investment organization that provides significant funding and strategic assistance to high-potential community-based organizations serving the core developmental, learning, and educational needs of children of low-income families in the National Capital Region.

While it is too early to make judgments on the overall value of the concept, the Morino Institute (2001) report offers this candid review of venture philanthropy:

- Venture philanthropy funds have continued to proliferate across a wide spectrum, ranging from highly engaged grant-making to simple capital allocation without any additional strategic assistance. It is premature to claim proof of concept for venture philanthropy because relatively few investments have been made and the grant recipients simply do not have measurable results yet.

- Many of the funds are so new, and have so few staff, that they will be challenged to build the capacity of any other nonprofit organization until they build their own capacity.

- The majority of nonprofit organizations are inexperienced in and unprepared for absorbing the kinds of strategic management support that venture philanthropists are tying to their financial investments. As a result, most grant recipients underestimate what is expected of them, and their organizations risk significant strain in executing their end of the partnership.

- There is still very little agreement about or utilization of metrics for success. Most funds promise to develop the measures in the future.

The Morino Institute report also says that "entrepeneurs, philanthropists, technology millionaires, and others are pulling philanthropy into the new millennium, holding it to higher standards, and imbuing it with strategies, techniques, and tools previously the private preserve of the venture capital world."

Not surprisingly, however, there are doubters. The problems that have arisen are varied. While the munificent size of most grants associated with venture philanthropists is enticing, the accompanying intrusive management advice and strict performance evaluation procedures have not been as welcome for some organizations. Face it, a major imbalance of power is introduced in any collaboration of the funding venture philanthropists and the beneficiary organization, especially for smaller community services.

Bruce Sievers, executive director of the Elise Haas Fund, is an outspoken critic of venture philanthropy. While maintaining there are important lessons to be gleaned from the for-profit world—mostly about management and operating efficiencies—Sievers (2000) finds "fundamental differences between the two kinds of human endeavor. Business and philanthropy . . . diverge in goals, aspirations, assumptions, and criteria of success. . . . There are fundamental areas in which business knowledge simply does not translate into social problem-solving and the nature and extent of these limits lies at the center of the 'venture capital debate.'" He suggests that venture philanthropists "are coming from a world where the way things get done is that you invest, hire bright people, kick butt, crush competition, take your money, and then go do something else. . . . That view doesn't necessarily apply to the nonprofit domain."

The strong emphasis of venture philanthropists on evaluation and managing for measured outcomes has both positive and negative impact. Nonprofit organizations must always drive for clear and objective evaluation of mission fulfillment and program performance; to the extent venture philanthropy furthers that end it must be welcomed. On the other hand, the outcomes of public service programs, by their very nature, are elusive and escape precise measures.

The application of clear financial reports by those from business used to directing their actions by them comes face-to-face with the ambiguity and qualitative judgments called for in determining performance of public service activities.

Susan Raymond (2000), chief analyst for Changing Our World, a philanthropic services company, puts it this way: "In sum, venture philanthropy seeks to hold social action and nonprofits to the same standards of performance that the new philanthropists themselves have had to meet to attract market venture capital and build the new burgeoning economy.

"The central problem of course is that the social problems addressed by much of the nation's not-for-profit infrastructure differ elementally from market opportunities. For some problems, root causes are not even clear, and hence strategic action and measurable results [are] difficult to design."

Keep this in mind, if you are a board member or executive: there may be a place for venture philanthropists to come in to your organization, underwrite its program, and help you govern and manage. There may be. But look carefully at all aspects.

Capacity Building

Capacity building, another currently fashionable concept, has come to mean a wide variety of things to different people.* To many the phrase is simply jargon and buzz. To others it is synonymous with technical assistance or organizational development.

The Environmental Support Center (2001) offers a useful definition of capacity building:

> Capacity building is any intentional work of an organization that gives it an increased ability to achieve its mission

*Much of this section is drawn from de Vita, C. J., and Fleming, C. (eds.), *Building Capacity in Nonprofit Organizations* (Urban Institute, 2001). Reprinted with permission.

and targets long-term organizational sustainability. Capacity building typically aims for internal operations, management, and administration rather than actual delivery of services or programmatic work. Things that fall under this umbrella, then, are things like strategic planning, leadership development, program development, fundraising, technology, human resource management, evaluation, accountability, media relations, membership development, marketing, and financial management. . . . Anything that allows your organization to operate more effectively internally is a part of capacity building.

So defined, it is hard to distinguish capacity building from sound governance and management that are the ever-present concern of nonprofit boards and executives—the Leadership Team of the organization.

However, if donor foundations and venture philanthropic organizations wish to walk the capacity-building path rather than traditional management formulations, nonprofit organizations can—indeed must—go along.

There is, moreover, a brighter side to capacity building. The interest that funders, particularly foundations, are showing in capacity building reflects a favorable turn to greater recognition that unrestricted support for operations, or restricted support for specific management needs, rather than exclusively programmatic funding, often can be the most helpful way of assisting a worthy nonprofit organization. As Backer and Bare (2000) point out, "All that buzz about capacity building boils down to a pretty simple premise: A strong, capable nonprofit organization stands a better chance of producing desired results than a weak one."

While sharing many similarities with venture philanthropy, the proponents of capacity building are markedly different in the manner of conveying assistance, notably in the lesser intrusion into the governance and management of the grantee organization. Foundations that want to help organizational competence across the range of management needs usually do so by underwriting the involvement of management support organizations or funding the employment of consultants to assist.

Remember this, if you are a board member or executive: welcome capacity building as a concept and an opportunity. Unless it is a rare exception, an organization can probably benefit from financial support directed at helping it strengthen its management functions, infrastructure, and operations that support the substantive mission of the organization. That is capacity building.

The whole sweep of management support functions fall in the range of capacity building. Foundations interested in making capacity-building grants may be interested in the whole of internal management operations, or in helping one or two programs that could result in a demonstrable difference in the organization fulfilling its mission.

Strategic planning, or technology, or fund raising are good examples. If some aspect of fund raising, such as direct mail or planned giving—or the program as a whole—needs a boost from outside in order to better the effectiveness of the whole organization, it may be ripe for a capacity-building grant. It calls for making a convincing case that help for these supporting activities is more important to the effectiveness of the organization, and more pressing, than direct programmatic support. That is capacity building.

Social Enterprise

Social enterprise is another concept getting wide attention that defies precise definition.

The Harvard Business School's whole program of management of nonprofit organizations and of for-profit businesses with a social purpose is called The Initiative on Social Enterprise. The mission of the Harvard program is

> To develop, adapt, and transfer management knowledge
> to catalyze excellence in leadership of nonprofit, private,

and public sector enterprises for the creation of social and economic value. . . . [It] seeks:

- To enhance the leadership, management, governance and entrepreneurial capabilities of social enterprises
- Strengthen the capacity and commitment of business leaders to interact effectively and positively with the larger society
- Advance the frontiers of knowledge about social enterprise
- Establish social enterprise as a recognized field of business scholarship

For some, social enterprise refers simply to nonprofits going into a money-raising business to raise funds to support their nonprofit, public service missions. Others see as social enterprise a business that, while clearly for-profit, has a basic purpose of doing good, such as to create jobs for the hard-to-employ or lending money at low rates to help struggling start-up ventures, especially in developing countries.

Social enterprise presents no prescribed forms, no definable programs. It is a concept board members and executives should be aware of, and they should take pride in the fact that, as nonprofit organizations, they are providing services with a social purpose and trust that they are showing enterprise in pursuing it.

Policy Governance Model

Consultant John Carver (1998), creator of the Policy Governance model, is quick to point out that his thesis is not a model in a true sense because, with the great variety of organizations, a genuinely applicable model of governance is impossible. Instead, he presents a set of "effectiveness characteristics" that can give rise to a "set of principles," a "theory of governance," a "system of board leadership."

Some of the features of the model are explored in the following discussion.*

- Policy clarification is the central element of board leadership. That means seeing policies in a more exacting light and developing them in terms of such categories as ends to be achieved, means to those ends, board-staff relationship, and the process of governance itself. With adherence to such policy categories, the revered practice of approving budgets, plans, and other administrative material—a process that cripples strategic leadership—becomes unnecessary.

- The focus of board wisdom should be on the most important issues (large ones, long-term ones, the most cogent ones), particularly the assurance of probity and explication of values.

- Those to whom responsibility is delegated must be allowed as much latitude as possible for decisions, creativity, and performance, while still ensuring board accountability for the total.

- The most important work of any governing body is to create and re-create the reason for organizational existence; that is, clarify and sustain the organization's mission.

- While a strong board needs a strong executive, more important than the selection of the executive is defining the relationship between the board and the

---

*Features are drawn from Carver, J., "Policy Governance Model: A Dialogue on Governance" (1998).

executive; it must be formed around the accountability of the position, not its responsibility.

The Policy Governance model has much to say about board committees: they are to help get the board's job done, not to help with the staff's job; they are to aid the process of governance, not management. Traditional committees are designed to be involved in staff-level issues; they are assigned tasks that essentially oversee, become involved in, or advise on management functions. As a result, it becomes less clear who is in charge of these activities. Thus, in the Policy Governance model it is difficult to justify personnel committees, executive committees, program committees, even finance committees, which tend to exist only to monitor staff performance.

"Legitimate" committees, rather than being tied to divisions of staff labor and topics, can be structured around the categories of policy-making; that is, board choices about ends, choices about executive limitations, policies about board process, and policies on the board-executive relationship.

Unquestionably the Policy Governance model has merit and, in its insistence that the board concentrate its efforts on ends, not means, and on forward-looking policymaking rather than close oversight of staff activities, it has value for nonprofit organizations across the board.

However, it must be noted that the model seems not to address one important function so critical to most nonprofit organizations: raising contributed funds. The board is vitally involved in this function; indeed the partnership of board and staff in the fund-raising activity, usually with a development committee, is inescapable.

Moreover, most nonprofit organizations find the budget process and general oversight of an organization's handling of finances involve important policy implications as well as the board's basic fiduciary responsibility, thus warranting an active finance committee. Likewise, in fulfilling its fiduciary role, the board cannot escape direct responsibility for the audit, which probably falls to the finance committee or a separate audit committee.

The model does acknowledge the probable need for a committee—essentially management as well as policy—when the board has retained to itself, as it should, responsibility for safeguarding endowment or reserve funds. Similarly, the model does respect the need for a nominating or governance committee that, while not helping the board create policy, is essential in recruiting its own membership.

Most boards therefore have need for some functional committees.

Boards and executives should find the principles underlying the model altogether worthy. The board's committee structure will need to be attuned to its particular needs, discussed in Chapter Eleven.

Boards—and executives—will be constantly challenged to watch for, understand, and be open-minded toward different management and governance concepts and models. They must judiciously pick and choose among them to select which ones, or which elements of any, can help in their organization and for their purposes.

16

Using Consultants

Consultants can be a boon or a bust. Bringing in an outsider with objectivity and knowledge of how similar organizations work can, at the right time and for the right purpose, be enormously helpful. On the other hand, enlisting consultative help for the wrong reason at the wrong time can prove to be unnervingly expensive and produce nothing not already known or that could be known without outside help.

Whichever way the dilemma is decided, the decision is important enough for the board to make it and to proceed in closest harmony with the executive and staff.

Some generalizations on consultants, often overlooked, should be kept in mind:

- Though cliché, it is no less true that consultants are paid to tell clients what they need to know, not what they want to hear.

- Consultants often can bring a fresh perspective to a traditional or everyday subject by relating the experience of similar organizations with the same problems and challenges.

- Consultants can serve an important role in bringing to a common purpose boards troubled by strongly held dissonant views, or boards and executives somewhat at odds.

- Consultants retained to perform duties normally performed by regular staff will usually be not only expensive but also less responsive to management direction. Furthermore, they can depart at any time, leaving an awkward gap.

- Often a foundation, less often a corporation or individual, can be found to underwrite a consultant fee when the outcome value can be persuasively shown. This is an aspect of capacity building.

There is plenty of advice available on using consultants. Here the discussion will be summary, supplemental to earlier chapters on specific governance and management functions and limited to only two dimensions: *whether to retain* a consultant and *how to use* a consultant.

Whether to Retain a Consultant

Some activities lend themselves to consultant assistance, others are marginal—helpful sometimes, for some purposes, for some organizations, but not always. Decisions on whether to retain a consultant relate to the different governance and management functions discussed in earlier chapters: executive recruitment, determination of mission—strategic planning, program evaluation, financial management, investments, fund raising, board development, application of information and communications tools, and marketing and public relations.

Executive Recruitment

Finding the right CEO, chief administrative or financial officer, or director of development can be the most critical problem facing an organization; you don't want to take chances. Finding candidates by word-of-mouth, advertising, and attendant interviews may be possible but also can be burdensome and chancy. The available market is filled with the less competent, the recently dismissed, and the inexperienced with beautiful resumes—all eager to respond to an ad. Especially for responsible board members in search of a CEO, or for CEOs seeking to fill key staff positions, sifting through and interviewing applicants can be time-consuming and frustrating.

Good search consultants will seek out candidates of proven capability, probably not looking for a change but attracted by a new opportunity that unexpectedly comes their way. Knowing the field and hiring routines, consultants can, with a professional eye, find the applicants, thoroughly review the resumes, do the intensive preliminary interviews, and present a selection of presumptively suitable candidates. Usually the consultant will guarantee the selection, which is to say, repeat the process at no charge if for valid reasons the candidate doesn't work out in the first year. All, of course, at a price—usually a healthy percentage of the first year's salary. The dilemma is this: Is it worth it? Can we afford it? Judgment hinges on the importance of the job and the affordability of the consultant.

A search for a CEO will of course be entirely in the hands of the board. A search for any staff member will be entirely in the hands of the executive, although board members may assist in obtaining a consultant.

Determination of Mission—Strategic Planning

Chapter Six points out that a comprehensive, board-approved articulation of an organization's mission is usually determined through a process of strategic planning. It emphasizes the importance of board ownership of the strategic planning process, the criticality of paying deliberate attention to the process, including making careful "plans for planning," and a preference for having an outside professional facilitator.

Such a facilitator or consultant brings a full understanding of the strategic planning processes, and, most important, in leading the strategic planning sessions can be objective and outcome-driven, allowing board leaders to participate fully, unencumbered with responsibility for leading the discussion.

Although the board owns the strategic planning process, a strategic planning facilitator can be retained by either the board or the executive; there should be full agreement between the board and executive on the consultant selection and the specifics of the job.

Program Evaluation

As Chapter Thirteen indicates, it is a tough call whether to enlist outside help in evaluating an organization's programs. It may well depend on the size of the organization, the depth of concern with how well the mission is being fulfilled, and whether programs are succeeding. It certainly makes a difference if a funder is willing to underwrite the process.

It is easy to lose sight of the difference between strategic planning—identifying national or community needs and providing programs to meet those needs—and program evaluation—assessing whether the organization is fulfilling its mission and programs are meeting national or community needs. The latter is far more demanding for an organization evaluating its own program or for a consultant leading an organization through the evaluation process.

Evaluating a public service, quite different from evaluating a for-profit business, has to lean on elusive, subjective criteria. There is a limited quantified, bottom-line base against which to make an evaluation; the judgments of so many varied constituencies are involved.

Since the outcome of a program evaluation is so critical to all they do, both the board and executive should be engaged in selecting consulting assistance. Use caution: consultants may claim to have the special expertise required but few are proven.

Financial Management

Not infrequently nonprofit organizations call in consultants to review financial operations and guide staff in the complexities of financial management and reporting, especially when complex personnel health and retirement benefits are involved.

In fulfilling their oversight responsibilities, boards may encourage or even insist on seeking financial consulting assistance.

Investments

Boards of nonprofit organizations with major endowments, reserve funds, or other income-earning assets will retain investment managers who, strictly speaking, are not consultants because, more than giving advice, they perform investment functions. However, evaluating the performance of outside investment managers—a highly desirable action, especially when large investment holdings are involved—requires the technical expertise of a consultant dedicated to that finely tuned process.

Boards are in charge of investments but executives can assist.

Fund Raising

The many aspects of fund-raising programs that can benefit from consultant assistance are reviewed in Chapter Ten. Notable are the following:

Development audits

Mass direct mail appeals

Proposal writing

Capital campaign feasibility studies

Planned-giving programs

Benefit events

Fund-raising accounting software

General assistance

The partnership of board and staff in fund raising dictates the need for full agreement in the retention of consulting assistance for any of the aspects of raising contributed funds.

Board Development

Boards, and executives assisting boards, often can use help in ensuring that the board is being fully effective in fulfilling its governance responsibilities and maintaining a strong organization and sound procedures. A consultant retained for what usually is referred to as board development can guide a board in thinking through just how it wants to organize itself and deal with its manifold activities and relationships.

Application of Information and Communications Tools

Consultants are widely and effectively used to help organizations adapt to the new information and communications technologies. Chapter Fourteen reviews four information and six communications tools that can have useful application to several governance and management functions. Consultants can help significantly in applying these tools and training employees in their use.

Marketing and Public Relations

In many nonprofit endeavors, public relations and marketing are central to attracting paying constituents—students, attendees of museums and performing arts, patients—on whom the organization's critically important earned revenues depend. Specialist consultants may prove beneficial, if not an absolute necessity, in achieving optimal performance in this activity.

The executive in charge of marketing may see the need for consulting help. In fulfilling their oversight, boards may encourage or even insist on seeking marketing consulting assistance.

How to Use a Consultant

Two considerations are important in using consultants: securing the *right consultant*, and *pinning down* the arrangement.

Securing the Right Consultant

Consultants often come to an organization by reference from another friendly organization that has used the consultant's services. That is healthy. But often, too, an organization has to go into the market; that is, through advertisements or professional lists find a selection of appropriate candidates from which to choose.

In walking this path, take all the care you would apply to hiring a key official. Don't automatically go for the readily available or someone a board member likes. Competitive bids not only will broaden the selection but will help in defining the project. Be sure first that the consultant has dealt with similar organizations with comparable subjects—fund raising, board development, personnel search. Always check references. Don't go on reputation alone. Reference checks must be thorough, not casual; the relationship is too important and expensive not to be taken very seriously. If possible, check with a previous client not listed as a reference by the prospective consultant.

Pinning Down the Arrangement

There is no great magic in it: when retaining a consultant, boards and executives first must be clear and agreed among themselves and then be in full agreement with the consultant on all aspects of the arrangement. The consultancy agreement or contract should be documented either with a proposal submitted by the consultant and agreed to by the organization, or, less formally, by a simple exchange of letters outlining the key elements.

The key elements or steps in a consultancy arrangement, on which board, staff, and consultant should be precisely clear, are straightforward without surprises. The following can be used as a checklist:

- The basic purpose of the consultancy
- The specific services to be provided

- The consultant firm's person or persons providing the services

- The time frame

- The report: when it will be submitted and what it will contain

- The fees, and what expenses will be reimbursed

- Termination clause: under what conditions either side can terminate the arrangement

Pitfalls

It is all too easy to slight the details in taking on a consultant and fail to come to a clear agreement on the elements in a consultancy arrangement.

As with employee performance, so with a consultant: it is easy when the performance is unquestionably good or clearly unsatisfactory; trouble comes when performance is marginal and you have to decide to accept the shortfall and go on from there or take difficult retributive steps. If at all possible, markers of achievement should be set out ahead of time in the basic agreement.

17

Special Challenges Facing the Leadership Team

The pitfalls that can arise in the management and governance of nonprofit organizations are discussed in several chapters. Of the more general, special challenges that can face the Leadership Team, three are discussed here:

- Being "businesslike"

- Unbalanced board and staff strengths

- "Founderitis"

These matters go to the heart of the way Leadership Teams function—the relationship among the board, chair, and the executive and staff; the roles of each; and how they get on together.

Being Businesslike

You will often hear it said, "Never forget, although you are a nonprofit charity, you are a business." And, "The more businesslike you are, the better it will be." Negative. You are better advised to keep reminding yourself, "You are a charity, a nonprofit, and *not* a business."

Being "businesslike" can mean a lot of different things. To many people it just stands for efficiency, for bottom-line discipline, for rigor. That isn't much help. Nonprofits can be efficient. Businesses can be inefficient. If it means using proven business procedures, it can have validity if the procedures are specified and the purposes made clear. In a word, business criteria should not be allowed to dominate the governance and management of nonprofit organizations.

Dennis R. Young (2000), president of the Association for Research on Nonprofit Organizations and Voluntary Action, puts it this way: "The 'reinvention' movement that developed in the halls of business and government . . . continues to knock at the doors of nonprofits. . . . But . . . strategies and solutions undertaken by organizations in other sectors were largely inappropriate for nonprofits. . . . The prescription that nonprofits should emulate business by becoming more entrepreneurial does not ring true to me. . . . The tenets of reinvention derived from business and government largely miss the mark for nonprofits."

Nonprofit management and governance practices differ markedly from those of business in fundamental purpose. Nonprofit organizations exist in large measure because there is no expectation of financial profit in their mission. Commercial companies, on the other hand, exist for the very purpose of creating an excess of revenues over expenses; that is, to make money for the owners.

While nonprofit organizations unquestionably must be financially responsible—they can't live on deficits—their underlying motivation is not to make money but rather to provide a service to the public, to their members, or to a cause. That difference in fundamental purpose is pervasive in the governance and management of nonprofits and therefore critical in the outlook, motivation, and performance of a nonprofit board and the executive and staff.

There is also a fundamental difference in income source. Business companies live on earnings from the sale of their products or services. While many nonprofit organizations depend heavily on earned revenues—tuitions, sales of admission tickets, hospital reimbursements, contracts and fees for service—in almost every case they rely on contributed funds for much if not all their financial resources. No business ever seeks contributions.

There are also differences in performance evaluation. As companies live by sales, so their performance is, quite properly, judged by a financial bottom line that can be precisely measured. Even though nonprofit organizations must live within their income, their performance is judged largely on their competence and the good they do—how well they fulfill their mission and achieve their public service, not by any financial measure.

Board members of nonprofit organizations are unpaid volunteers; those on business boards are paid, often quite handsomely. Business board members answer to their owners—the stockholders; nonprofit board members are trustees and answer to the public and to their own consciences. For good reason boards of business companies are small and efficient. For equally good reason boards of nonprofit organizations are larger; they are effective among other reasons because they seek out diversity, participation of their constituencies, and the skills demanded of nonprofit governance. Effectiveness is thus not a matter of efficiency but rather how well they do their job in leading the organization to respond to a community need.

These differences having been noted, there should be no question that nonprofit boards and executives can use business principles and procedures as models in financial management and marketing.

Unbalanced Board and Staff Strengths

Leadership Teams can be out of balance. A board can fall short in its governing responsibility, distant and detached from the operations of the organization, or it can be too aggressive—micromanaging—in overseeing the executive. The executive can be too dominant, usurping the board's role in major policy determinations, or, as manager, be too submissive.

Size can make a difference in the normal balance. The president of a university and the director of a major museum are expected to assume dominant leadership roles, assuming many of the responsibilities usually accorded the board, albeit with the board retaining final word on major financial decisions. On the other hand, small, start-up community service organizations frequently come into existence through a few enthusiastic volunteers who manage and govern the organization as its only workers until it matures enough to take on an executive and paid staff.

Large national organizations with regional chapters or affiliates present a special problem. Often local boards, possibly composed of worker volunteers, manage as well as govern. On the other hand, regional chapters, such as in environmental organizations and large healthcare nonprofits can have an executive director so strong and assertive as to appear indispensable and thus reduce the board to subservience.

Solutions—bringing about a balance in board and staff leadership strengths—depend inevitably on personalities. No single pattern works in the personal relations among the chair, the executive, and strong board members—their compatibilities and willingness to compromise and adjust. Together they need to recognize the problem, accommodate, and get back to the basic lines of governance and management.

Founderitis

"Founderitis" is a disease that can inflict the Leadership Team of an organization large or small and may be hard to cure. The founder of a major national organization stays on the board, though perhaps no longer its chair, and continues to dominate the proceedings. He resists change: "If it ain't broke, don't fix it."

Or the founding executive of a successful community organization selects the board, mostly her friends, and for years virtually makes all the decisions. She won't let go.

What can you do? In the case of a founding board chair, term limits and rotation for board membership and officer positions are the best solutions, but they may be difficult to introduce if they are not already in place. It pays also to be guarded in awarding emeritus and life board memberships that can complicate an existing problem.

For the executive who may have started an organization and hangs on, the only answer is to develop a strong board that can retrieve the balance of leadership.

> *It is inescapable: one of the true tests of leadership of a board chair or an executive is to arrange for orderly succession.*

18

Accountability

Every nonprofit organization, because it is supported by public contributions and given favorable treatment by tax laws, is accountable to the public.

In light of recent prominent scandals where major charitable organizations have failed in their public trust, accountability takes on a special importance and is getting a lot of public attention. Had the boards and executives of those organizations been fully accountable, distress would not have been visited upon them; indeed the entire philanthropic community would have avoided considerable stress and distress.

But who is accountable, and to whom? And for what are they accountable?

First the who. Since the board is ultimately responsible for the whole organization and all that it does, the buck stops with the board; it is the locus of accountability. The executive, playing a major part in the operation of an organization, inevitably is a key factor in accountability, but the executive is accountable to the board.

Note: This chapter is adapted from an article that appeared in the November/ December 2000 issue of *Nonprofit World*, a journal of the Society of Nonprofit Organizations, and later in *Nonprofit Governance and Management* (2002), an edition of the American Society of Corporate Secretaries and the Section of Business Law of the American Bar Association. The material is used with permission.

Accountable to whom? The attorney general in each state has a general but often not clearly defined oversight responsibility for non-profit organizations. The Internal Revenue Service wields authority through its tax exemption authority. But the accountability of non-profit organizations is principally to the public—a formless entity to which boards somehow owe a fiduciary answerability. In large measure, therefore, unless things go awry, boards and board members answer to their own consciences before the public and to their own self-determined principles of what is right and good.

Turn then to what the board is accountable for. In essence, accountability is a matter of three interactive elements: performance reliability, integrity through openness, and standards and codes of excellence.

Performance Reliability

A nonprofit organization stands accountable for its performance in the following dimensions: *financial integrity*, right and proper *fund raising*, *program performance*, and the *board's own performance*.

- *Financial accountability*. The board's watch over the organization's financial integrity, reviewed in Chapter Eight, has many facets. The most important long-term tool in its accountability for financial integrity rests in the audit, the instrument on which the board should put unrelenting emphasis. The board's involvement in the budget is also integral to its accountability. Close oversight of the organization's finances by a budget and finance committee and regular board review of the budget and the "financials" are the most important day-to-day ways of maintaining controls and ensuring financial integrity.
- *Fund-raising accountability*. A part of the board's role for which it is accountable, separate from the financial, is fund raising, the oversight and participation in attracting the contributed resources to sustain programs discussed in Chapter Ten. The board has to be as-

sured the organization's various ways of raising money conform to well-known and acceptable practices.

• *Program performance accountability.* Watching over programs touches on many matters discussed in several chapters. Clarity of mission—the purposes, programs, and priorities of the organization, and the vision for its future—discussed in Chapter Six, are front and center in the board's accountability. So too is the board's program oversight, discussed in Chapter Seven, and especially program evaluation, discussed in Chapter Thirteen.

• *Board effectiveness.* The board's answerability for its own performance incorporates the matters raised in Chapter Eleven—notably, the fulfillment of its governance responsibilities and the effectiveness of its own organization and procedures, all of which also involve the executive.

Integrity Through Openness

A central part of board accountability—fulfilling its fiduciary responsibility—is for it to be fully open to public scrutiny: to make public its financial statements, available in its IRS Form 990; to be especially guarded against conflicts of interest in board members and staff; and generally not to hide its problems.

To put it the other way, a board and executive that keep the organization's performance to itself, wrapped in secrecy, is presumably breaching the fiduciary responsibility for full accountability—and therefore is suspect.

Standards and Codes

A number of so-called watchdog groups—some nonprofit, others for-profit agencies—have established standards for public accountability, use of funds, informational materials, fund-raising practices, and governance. These agencies regularly review organizations and issue statements on their conformity to the standards, or are

retained by donors of major grants to check out recipient institutions. The standards for charitable accountability of the well-known
nonprofit Council of Better Business Bureau's Wise Giving Alliance
are seen in Resource E.

In addition, at least two private state associations of nonprofit
organizations have issued comprehensive standards for excellence
dealing with ethics and accountability: Maryland Association of
Nonprofit Organizations (2003, Web site: mdnonprofit.org) and
Minnesota Council of Nonprofits (2003, Web site: mncn.org). They
too are fully available.

Summary

Accountability of the board of a nonprofit organization, and of the
executive through the board, is the beginning and end of what
constitutes the role of the Leadership Team and what it stands for.
The biggest and most pervasive demand upon the Leadership Team
is to recognize and accept in all its governance and management
responsibilities the need to be open and fully accountable for all
that it does.

Accountability thus relates to each of the responsibilities of the
board in its governance and of the executive in management, and
of their joint responsibilities as the Leadership Team that this book
is all about:

- The mission and vision of the organization that the
  board and staff jointly devise and direct programs
  to fulfill

- The deliberate, thoughtful, and thorough
  program evaluations to ensure fulfillment of the
  mission

- The financial viability and integrity that board and
  staff go to great lengths to uphold

- The responsible, ethical, and productive fund raising on which the organization's programs rely

- The assurance that both the board and the executive are fully effective and open in fulfilling their governance and management responsibilities

Accountability is not one chapter or one subject, it is the total message.

Conclusion

Some will read straight through this book, though not in one sitting, seeking to grasp the whole, the many and mixed elements that make for a strong Leadership Team. Others will find its value as a reference, turning to certain chapters when the course of governance and management of their nonprofit organization brings up a question how to deal with one of the many challenges that face the leaders. May it bring some useful perspective, some source of strength, to both.

When boards and executives work well as a team, the organization will be strong. But even more, they will find the immense satisfaction that comes from working together for a set of values and helping their organization make a significant contribution to the community in which they live.

Resources

Resource A

CompassPoint Board-Staff "Contract" for Financial Accountability

Related to Tax and Legal Responsibilities,

The staff will:	The board will:
Immediately notify the board with complete information related to any delays in payroll tax payments or any legal matters; Immediately notify the board of any tax problems or penalties; and Immediately notify the board of any legal suits.	Work closely with staff to respond to notification of possible tax problems and develop plans for resolving tax and legal problems; and Formally approve any tax and legal settlements.

Related to Accounting,

The staff will:	The board will:
Complete monthly or quarterly statements within	Form a Finance Committee of members that understand

Source: CompassPoint Nonprofit Services, San Francisco, Calif., 2003. Reprinted with permission.

Related to Accounting,

The staff will:	The board will:
three weeks of the end of the month: Income and expense statement for each major program and for the organization as a whole (should include statements for the previous month and on a year-to-date basis); Balance sheet for the organization as a whole; For large organizations with substantial restricted funds and/or an endowment fund, a balance sheet for the restricted funds; and Comparison of actual to budget on a year-to-date basis for the organization and, if appropriate, for each program. Mail statements to Finance Committee in advance of meeting. If the statements are not available, explain the delay and estimate a date by which the statements will be completed. In a timely manner, prepare end-of-year statements, Federal Form 990 and other federal and state forms.	financial information and standard accounting terms and practices; Carefully read financial information; Ask questions to be sure the statements are understood; Periodically review key accounting policies, such as depreciation, cash or accrual basis statements, etc.; and Be patient and understanding when statements are occasionally late or infrequent; accounting problems occur.

In Cash Flow Projections,

The staff will:	The board will:
If appropriate for the organization, prepare monthly, quarterly, or annual cash flow projection;	Pay attention to cash flow reports; and
If appropriate, prepare a comparison of actual to projected cash flows;	Determine whether preparation of cash flow reports provides important enough information to justify the staff time required.
If cash flow shortages are projected, develop a plan for bridging the shortages; and	
If cash flow surpluses are projected, develop a plan for maximizing investment.	

In Financial Analysis,

The staff will:	The board will:
Prepare brief written narrative monthly or quarterly including the following:	Propose items for ad hoc investigation;
Highlights of recent period;	Discuss analyses with staff; work with staff to improve financial performance; and
Outstanding and/or anticipated problems;	
Anticipated opportunities;	In the absence of the expertise on staff, one or more individual board members may be able to do some of the analysis.
Analysis of financial health; and	
Comments on recent financial performance.	
As part of the annual budget preparation or at another key juncture:	

In Financial Analysis (cont.)

The staff will:	The board will:
Investigate and analyze outside trends affecting the organization's finances;	
Revisit key decisions related to assets and liabilities, such as mortgages, debt, investments; and	
Prepare vertical and, if possible, horizontal analyses.	

In Relation to the Audit and Internal Controls,

The staff will:	The board will:
If audited, ensure that audited statements and management letter are completed within four months of the end of the fiscal year;	Determine whether or not an audit is appropriate;
	Take the lead in interviewing prospective auditors and review of bids;
Prepare a written response to comments and recommendations in the management letter; and	Select the auditor;
	Meet at least once per year with auditor when no staff is present;
Develop a written set of internal controls and follow procedures in spirit as well as to the letter.	Receive audit letter directly from auditor; and
	Review written internal control procedures.

In Relation to the Budget,

The staff will:	The board will:
Develop a proposed budget by program and for the organization as a whole; Be given the authority to make minor changes (such as shifting dollars among line items, or increases in variable costs that are matched by increases in earned revenue) in the budget without board approval; and If significant budget variances occur, explain the variances and proposed action such as better attention to budget control or revised end-of-year projections.	Develop parameters for staff to guide preparation of the draft budget, such as maximum allowable deficit for the year, reduction of Accounts Payable, etc.; Give careful attention to budget reports; Engage in long-term planning for funding, such as identifying a target mix of contributed and earned monies; and Formally accept the budget, thereby authorizing the beginning of operations as planned.

In Salaries and Personnel,

The staff will:	The board will:
Prepare an annual schedule showing each staff person and that person's salary for the Finance Committee and/or Personnel Committee; and Prepare an annual schedule of individuals to whom 1099s were issued, and the amounts.	Establish salary ranges for each category of employee; Approve guidelines for performance-based compensation, if appropriate; Negotiate and approve the executive director's salary; Ensure that other salaries are within approved salary ranges, or if not, to have approved exceptions;

In Salaries and Personnel (cont.)

The staff will:	The board will:
	Approve personnel policies; and
	Periodically review employee benefits.

In General,

The staff will:	The board will:
Make a good faith effort to communicate all significant information;	Give serious attention to financial information;
Ungrudgingly complete requests for ad hoc reports;	Be understanding when problems occur;
Appreciate that tough questions are appropriate and not hostile;	Make only reasonable requests for ad hoc reports;
Have good answers.	Work as problem solvers as well as governors;
	Be willing to ask "tough" questions;
	Respect the difficulty of the work, and express appreciation when appropriate;
	Ask good questions.

Resource B

Committee on Trustees or Governance Committee
Sample Terms of Reference

The governance committee (or committee on trustees) shall be responsible for making nominations for membership on the board, and for its officers, in accordance with the by-laws. In addition, the committee will keep under constant review the manner in which the board itself fulfills its responsibilities and conducts its business, in order to make recommendations to the board on its effectiveness. Accordingly, it will review and make recommendations on such matters, among others, as the by-laws; board committee structure and membership; decision-making processes; meetings, agendas, procedures, and schedules; board-staff relations; conflicts of interest; evaluation of board members; new board member orientation; and such other matters as it believes will contribute to the effectiveness of the board or are referred to it by the chairperson or president.

Resource C

Board Self-Assessment for Nonprofit Organizations
Some Guiding Principles

1. The basic assumption is that the effectiveness of the board of a nonprofit organization is a major part of the effectiveness of the organization.

2. The fundamental purpose of board self-assessment is for the board periodically and constructively to ensure the integrity, care, and skill in its fulfillment of its responsibilities and to seek constantly to improve its procedures to maintain its effectiveness.

3. Board self-assessment can only be successful if board members want it, accept the foregoing basic assumption, and proceed with the assessment when no higher authority requires it and despite the sensitivity of such assessments and interference they cause with handling of other pressing business.

4. Boards can carry out self-assessments in a number of different ways, not mutually exclusive:

   a. Using a standing committee on trustees, or governance committee, to keep board effectiveness under constant review.

   b. Having a regular meeting agenda item to discuss board procedures and effectiveness.

   c. Inviting an outside professional to brief the board on conducting self-assessments.

    d. Carrying out on its own a survey of board member views on the various elements of board effectiveness.

    e. Retaining professional counsel to assist in the board self-assessment, in a sense making a board effectiveness audit, involving methods of survey, personal interviews, facilitating board discussions, and recommendations.

5. The outcomes of successful board self-assessments will be a demonstrable, stepped-up awareness of the elements of board effectiveness on the part of the members, and a reaffirmation of board organization and procedures, or agreement on specific changes to improve board governance of the organization.

Resource D

ePhilanthropy Code of Ethical Online Philanthropic Practices

ePhilanthropyFoundation.Org exists to foster the effective and safe use of the Internet for philanthropic purposes. In its effort to promote high ethical standards in online fundraising and to build trust among contributors in making online transactions and contributions with the charity of their choice, this code is being offered as a guide to all who share this goal. Contributors are encouraged to be aware of non-internet related fundraising practices that fall outside the scope of this Code.

Ethical Online Practices and Practitioners will:

Section A: Philanthropic Experience

1. Clearly and specifically display and describe the organization's identity on the organization's Web site.

2. Employ practices on the Web site that exhibit integrity, honesty, and truthfulness and seek to safeguard the public trust.

Section B: Privacy and Security

1. Seek to inspire trust in every online transaction.

2. Prominently display the opportunity for supporters to have their names removed from lists that are sold to, rented to, or exchanged with other organizations.

Source: ePhilanthropyFoundation.Org, July 2002. Reprinted with permission.

3. Conduct online transactions through a system that employs high-level, security technology, to protect the donor's personal information; for both internal and external authorized use.

4. Provide either an "opt in" and "opt out" mechanism to prevent unsolicited communications or solicitations by organizations that obtain email addresses directly from the donor. Should lists be rented or exchanged only those verified, as having been obtained through donors or prospects "opting in" will be used by a charity.

5. Protect the interests and privacy of individuals interacting with their Web site.

6. Provide a clear, prominent and easily accessible privacy policy on its Web site telling visitors, at a minimum, what information is being collected, how this information will be used and who has access to the data.

Section C: Disclosures

1. Disclose the identity of the organization or provider processing an online transaction.

2. Guarantee that the name, logo and likeness of all parties to an online transaction belong to the party and will not be used without express permission.

3. Maintain all appropriate governmental and regulatory designations or certifications.

Section D: Complaints

1. Provide protection to hold the donor harmless of any problem arising from a transaction conducted through the organization's Web site.

2. Promptly respond to all customer complaints and employ best efforts to fairly resolve all legitimate complaints in a timely fashion.

Section E: Transactions

1. Insure contributions are used to support the activities of the organization to which they were donated.

2. Insure that legal control of contributions or proceeds from online transactions are transferred directly to the charity or expedited in the fastest possible way.

3. Companies providing online services to charities will provide clear and full communication with the charity on all aspects of donor transactions including the accurate and timely transmission of data related to online transactions.

4. Stay informed regarding the best methods to insure the ethical, secure and private nature of online ePhilanthropy transactions.

5. Adhere to the spirit as well as the letter of all applicable laws and regulations, including but not limited to charity solicitation and tax laws.

6. Insure that all services, recognition and other transactions promised on a Web site, in consideration of gift or transaction, will be fulfilled on a timely basis.

7. Disclose to the donor the nature of the relationship between the organization processing the gift or transaction and the charity intended to benefit from the gift.

ePhilanthropyFoundation.Org (2001, 2002)
1101 15th Street, NW
Suite 200
Washington, DC 20005
www.ePhilanthropyFoundation.org
Approved: November 12, 2000
Revised: January 25, 2001, September 23, 2002

Resource E

BBB Wise Giving Alliance Standards for Charitable Accountability

Preface

The BBB Wise Giving Alliance Standards for Charitable Accountability were developed to assist donors in making sound giving decisions and to foster public confidence in charitable organizations. The standards seek to encourage fair and honest solicitation practices, to promote ethical conduct by charitable organizations and to advance support of philanthropy.

These standards replace the separate standards of the National Charities Information Bureau and the Council of Better Business Bureaus' Foundation and its Philanthropic Advisory Service that were in place at the time the organizations merged.

The Standards for Charitable Accountability were developed with professional and technical assistance from representatives of small and large charitable organizations, the accounting profession, grant making foundations, corporate contributions officers, regulatory agencies, research organizations and the Better Business Bureau

Note: Copyright 2003. Reprinted with the permission of BBB Wise Giving Alliance. BBB Wise Giving Alliance is a merger of the National Charities Information Bureau and the Council of Better Business Bureaus' Foundation and its Philanthropic Advisory Service. BBB Wise Giving Alliance, 4200 Wilson Blvd., Suite 600, Arlington, Va. 22209, www.give.org.

system. The BBB Wise Giving Alliance also commissioned significant independent research on donor expectations to ensure that the views of the general public were reflected in the standards.

The generous support of the Charles Stewart Mott Foundation, the Surdna Foundation, and Sony Corporation of America helped underwrite the development of these standards and related research.

Organizations that comply with these accountability standards have provided documentation that they meet basic standards:

- In how they govern their organization,

- In the ways they spend their money,

- In the truthfulness of their representations, and

- In their willingness to disclose basic information to the public.

These standards apply to publicly soliciting organizations that are tax exempt under section 501(c)(3) of the Internal Revenue Code and to other organizations conducting charitable solicitations. The standards are not intended to apply to private foundations, as they do not solicit contributions from the public.

The overarching principle of the BBB Wise Giving Alliance Standards for Charitable Accountability is full disclosure to donors and potential donors at the time of solicitation and thereafter. However, where indicated, the standards recommend ethical practices beyond the act of disclosure in order to ensure public confidence and encourage giving. As voluntary standards, they also go beyond the requirements of local, state and federal laws and regulations.

In addition to the specific areas addressed in the standards, the BBB Wise Giving Alliance encourages charitable organizations to adopt the following management practices to further the cause of charitable accountability.

- Initiate a policy promoting pluralism and diversity within the organization's board, staff, and constituencies. While organizations vary widely in their ability to demonstrate pluralism and diversity, every organization should establish a policy, consistent with its mission statement, that fosters such inclusiveness.

- Ensure adherence to all applicable local, state and federal laws and regulations including submission of financial information.

- Maintain an organizational adherence to the specific standards cited below. The BBB Wise Giving Alliance also encourages charities to maintain an organizational commitment to accountability that transcends specific standards and places a priority on openness and ethical behavior in the charity's programs and activities.

Standards for Charitable Accountability

Governance and Oversight

The governing board has the ultimate oversight authority for any charitable organization. This section of the standards seeks to ensure that the volunteer board is active, independent and free of self-dealing. To meet these standards, the organization shall have:

1. **A board of directors that provides adequate oversight of the charity's operations and its staff.** Indication of adequate oversight includes, but is not limited to, regularly scheduled appraisals of the CEO's performance, evidence of disbursement controls such as board approval of the budget, fund raising practices, establishment of a conflict of interest policy, and establishment of accounting procedures sufficient to safeguard charity finances.

2. **A board of directors with a minimum of five voting members.**

3. **A minimum of three evenly spaced meetings per year of the full governing body with a majority in attendance, with face-to-face participation.** A conference call of the full board can substitute for one of the three meetings of the governing body. For all meetings, alternative modes of participation are acceptable for those with physical disabilities.

4. **Not more than one or 10% (whichever is greater) directly or indirectly compensated person(s) serving as voting member(s) of the board. Compensated members shall not serve as the board's chair or treasurer.**

5. **No transaction(s) in which any board or staff members have *material* conflicting interests with the charity resulting from any relationship or business affiliation.** Factors that will be considered when concluding whether or not a related party transaction constitutes a conflict of interest and if such a conflict is material, include, but are not limited to: any arm's length procedures established by the charity; the size of the transaction relative to like expenses of the charity; whether the interested party participated in the board vote on the transaction; if competitive bids were sought and whether the transaction is one-time, recurring or ongoing.

Measuring Effectiveness

An organization should regularly assess its effectiveness in achieving its mission. This section seeks to ensure that an organization has defined, measurable goals and objectives in place and a defined process in place to evaluate the success and impact of its program(s) in fulfilling the goals and objectives of the organization and that also identifies ways to address any deficiencies. To meet these standards, a charitable organization shall:

6. Have a board policy of assessing, no less than every two years, the organization's performance and effectiveness and of determining future actions required to achieve its mission.

7. Submit to the organization's governing body, for its approval, a written report that outlines the results of the aforementioned performance and effectiveness assessment and recommendations for future actions.

Finances

This section of the standards seeks to ensure that the charity spends its funds honestly, prudently and in accordance with statements made in fund raising appeals. To meet these standards, the charitable organization shall:

(Please note that standards 8 and 9 have *different* denominators.)

8. **Spend at least 65% of its total expenses on program activities.**

9. **Spend no more than 35% of *related* contributions on fund raising.** Related contributions include donations, legacies, and other gifts received as a result of fund raising efforts.

10. **Avoid accumulating funds that could be used for current program activities. To meet this standard, the charity's unrestricted net assets available for use should not be more than three times the size of the past year's expenses or three times the size of the current year's budget, whichever is higher.**

   An organization that does not meet Standards 8, 9 and/or 10 may provide evidence to demonstrate that its use of funds is reasonable. The higher fund raising and administrative costs of a newly created organization, donor restrictions on the use of funds, exceptional bequests, a stigma associated with a cause and environmental or political events beyond an

organization's control are among factors which may result in expenditures
that are reasonable although they do not meet the financial measures cited
in these standards.

11. **Make available to all, on request, complete annual financial**
    statements prepared in accordance with generally accepted
    accounting principles. When total annual gross income
    exceeds $250,000, these statements should be audited in
    accordance with generally accepted auditing standards. For
    charities whose annual gross income is less than $250,000, a
    review by a certified public accountant is sufficient to meet
    this standard. For charities whose annual gross income is less
    than $100,000, an internally produced, complete financial
    statement is sufficient to meet this standard.

12. **Include in the financial statements a breakdown of**
    expenses (e.g., salaries, travel, postage, etc.) that shows
    what portion of these expenses was allocated to program,
    fund raising, and administrative activities. If the charity has
    more than one major program category, the schedule should
    provide a breakdown for each category.

13. **Accurately report the charity's expenses, including any**
    joint cost allocations, in its financial statements. For
    example, audited or unaudited statements which inaccurately
    claim zero fund raising expenses or otherwise understate the
    amount a charity spends on fund raising, and/or overstate
    the amount it spends on programs will not meet this standard.

14. **Have a board-approved annual budget for its current fiscal**
    year, outlining projected expenses for major program
    activities, fund raising, and administration.

Fund Raising and Information Materials

A fund raising appeal is often the only contact a donor has with a char-
ity and may be the sole impetus for giving. This section of the standards
seeks to ensure that a charity's representations to the public are accurate,

complete and respectful. To meet these standards, the charitable organization shall:

15. **Have solicitations and information materials, distributed by any means, that are accurate, truthful and not misleading, both in whole and in part.** Appeals that omit a clear description of program(s) for which contributions are sought will not meet this standard.

    A charity should also be able to substantiate that the timing and nature of its expenditures are in accordance with what is stated, expressed, or implied in the charity's solicitations.

16. **Have an annual report available to all, on request, that includes:**
    a. the organization's mission statement,
    b. a summary of the past year's program service accomplishments,
    c. a roster of the officers and members of the board of directors,
    d. financial information that includes (i) total income in the past fiscal year, (ii) expenses in the same program, fund raising and administrative categories as in the financial statements, and (iii) ending net assets.

17. **Include on any charity websites that solicit contributions, the same information that is recommended for annual reports, as well as the mailing address of the charity and electronic access to its most recent IRS Form 990.**

18. **Address privacy concerns of donors by**
    a. providing in written appeals, at least annually, a means (e.g., such as a check off box) for both new and continuing donors to inform the charity if they do not want their name and address shared outside the organization, and
    b. providing a clear, prominent and easily accessible privacy policy on any of its websites that tells visitors (i) what

information, if any, is being collected about them by the charity and how this information will be used, (ii) how to contact the charity to review personal information collected and request corrections, (iii) how to inform the charity (e.g., a check off box) that the visitor does not wish his/her personal information to be shared outside the organization, and (iv) what security measures the charity has in place to protect personal information.

19. **Clearly disclose how the charity benefits from the sale of products or services (i.e., cause-related marketing) that state or imply that a charity will benefit from a consumer sale or transaction. Such promotions should disclose, at the point of solicitation:**
    a. the actual or anticipated portion of the purchase price that will benefit the charity (e.g., 5 cents will be contributed to abc charity for every xyz company product sold),
    b. the duration of the campaign (e.g., the month of October),
    c. any maximum of guaranteed minimum contribution amount (e.g., up to a maximum of $200,000).

20. **Respond promptly to and act on complaints brought to its attention by the BBB Wise Giving Alliance and/or local Better Business Bureaus about fund raising practices, privacy policy violations and/or other issues.**

References

Allison, M. "Into the Fire: Boards and Executive Transitions." *Nonprofit Management and Leadership*, Summer 2002, *12*(4).

Axelrod, N. R. *Chief Executive Succession Planning*. Washington, D.C.: BoardSource, 2002a.

Axelrod, N. R. "Don't Be Known as Enron U." *Trusteeship*, July/Aug. 2002b.

BBB Wise Giving Alliance. *Standards for Charitable Accountability, 2003*. Arlington, Va.: Better Business Bureaus, 2003 (available on-line at www.give.org).

Backer, T. E., and Bare, J. "Going to the Next Level." *Foundation News and Commentary*, Sept./Oct. 2000.

Campbell, D. "Outcomes Assessment and the Paradox of Nonprofit Accountability." *Nonprofit Management and Leadership*, Spring 2002, *12*(4).

Carver, J. *Boards That Make a Difference*. San Francisco: Jossey-Bass, 1990.

Carver, J. "Policy Governance Model: A Dialogue on Governance." NCNB National Leadership Forum, 1998.

Chait, R. P. *How to Help Your Board Govern More and Manage Less*. Washington, D.C.: BoardSource, 1998.

Chronicle of Philanthropy. "Philanthropy 400." Oct. 31, 2002 (entire issue).

Coastal Enterprise. *Annual Report*. Wiscasset, Maine: 2002.

CompassPoint Nonprofit Services. *Board-Staff "Contract" for Financial Accountability, 2003*.

de Vita, C. J., and Fleming, C. (eds.). *Building Capacity in Nonprofit Organizations*. Washington, D.C.: Urban Institute, 2001.

Environmental Support Center. "Capacity Building Defined." *Resources*, Winter 2001.

Enzer, M. *Matisse's Glossary of Internet Terms*, 2000 (available on-line at www.matisse.net/files/glossary.html).

ePhilanthropy Foundation. ePhilanthropy Code of Ethical Practices, Newsletter of the American Institute of Philanthropy, July 2002 (available at ePhilanthropyFoundation.org).

Espy, S. N. *Marketing Strategy for Nonprofit Organizations*. Chicago, Ill.: Lyceum Books, 1993.

Etzioni, A. "When It Comes to Ethics, B-Schools Get an F." *Washington Post*, Aug. 4, 2002.

Fine, A. H. "Charities Must Prove That They Get Results." *Chronicle of Philanthropy*, June 10, 1997.

Fix, J. L. "A Charity Stops the Presses." *Chronicle of Philanthropy*, Aug. 9, 2001.

Frantzreb, A. C. *Not on This Board You Don't*. Chicago, Ill.: Bonus Books, 1996.

Frumkin, P. "Going Beyond Efficiency." *Nonprofit Quarterly*, July 2001.

Maryland Association of Nonprofit Organizations, 2003 (mdnonprofit.org) and Minnesota Council of Nonprofits, 2003 (mncn.org).

Masaoka, J. "A Board-Staff 'Contract' for Financial Accountability." *Board Café* (CompassPoint), Nov. 2000.

Masaoka, J. "Support Your Local Executive Director." *Board Café* (Compass-Point), June 2002.

Masaoka, J., and Allison, M. "Why Boards Don't Govern." *Boardmember*, Washington, D.C.: National Center for Nonprofit Boards, Mar. 1998.

Moffet, C. "Effective Technology Is Mission-Based Technology." *WCA Nonprofit Agenda*, Jan./Feb. 2002.

Morino Institute. *Venture Philanthropy: The Changing Landscape*. Morino Institute: Reston, Va.: 2001.

Nardick, D. "Time to Move Beyond Intrastructure." *Technos Quarterly* (Journal of the Agency for Instructional Technology), Nov. 2002, *11*(3).

Raymond, S. *Venture Philanthropy: An Idea, But Is It a Good Idea?* Changing Our World Inc., 2000.

Robinson, M. K. *The Chief Executive's Role in Developing the Nonprofit Board*. BoardSource Governance Series, 1998.

Ryan, W. "Financial Responsibility of Boards." *Nonprofit Quarterly*, Apr. 2001.

Sievers, B. "Lost in Translation: What 'Venture Philanthropy' Can Teach and What It Has to Learn." *Philanthropy*, Nov./Dec. 2000.

Soder, R. *The Language of Leadership*. San Francisco: Jossey-Bass, 2001.

Szanton, P. *Board Assessment of the Organization*. BoardSource Governance Series, 1998.

Taylor, B. E., Chait, R. P., and Holland, T. P. "The New Work of the Nonprofit Board." *Harvard Business Review,* Sept./Oct. 1996.

Venture Philanthropy Partners. *Investing in Social Change.* Washington, D.C.: Venture Philanthropy Partners, 2001.

Young, D. R. "President's Message." *Association for Research on Nonprofit Organizations and Voluntary Action News,* Spring 2000.

Index